Aquaponics
Q and A

The answers to your questions
about aquaponics

Dr. James Rakocy

Photos, book design
by Rebecca L. Nelson

Aquaponics Q and A

By Dr. James Rakocy

Copyright © 2011 - all rights reserved

Nelson and Pade, Inc.

Published by:

Nelson and Pade, Inc.

PO Box 761, Montello, WI USA 53949

Email: info@aquaponics.com

Web: www.aquaponics.com, www.aquaponicsjournal.com

ISBN 978-0-9779696-3-0

Printed in the USA

Disclaimer: Publisher, Nelson and Pade, Inc. and author, Dr. James Rakocy, have made every attempt to provide accurate and timely information in this book. However, the information and technical data within may not match your circumstances and constitutes an approximate guide only. The success of any aquaponic systems is solely the responsibility of the owner and operator, and not that of Nelson and Pade, Inc. or Dr. James Rakocy.

Table of Contents

Foreword

By Rebecca L. Nelson
Editor, Aquaponics Journal

Dr. James Rakocy earned his PhD in aquaculture from Auburn University in Alabama and from 1980 - 2010, worked as the Agricultural Experiment Station Director and Research Professor of Aquaculture at the University of the Virgin Islands (UVI) in St. Croix. Dr. Rakocy is the world's foremost research scientist in aquaponics and is known around the world for his contributions to the development of aquaponic technology.

When I met Dr. Rakocy at UVI shortly after we began publishing the Aquaponics Journal in 1997, I was inspired and a bit awed by his achievements in aquaponics and aquaculture. In subsequent conversations and interviews I had the opportunity to get to know Dr. Rakocy and leaned that he, too, was a Wisconsin native and his passion for fish started when he was very young, with an abundance of aquariums in his boyhood home in Milwaukee and many of his summer days spent angling for bluegills in local lakes.

A few years after first meeting Dr. Rakocy, as the Aquaponics Journal subscriber base was growing along with the global interest in aquaponics, I asked him if he would be willing to contribute to each issue, answering reader questions in the Q and A column. He graciously accepted and has since written this column in every issue, often doing so under pressure from multiple unrelated deadlines and responsibilities.

Over the years, the Q and A column has become an incredible resource for anyone looking for detailed answers to questions in aquaponics. I've referred to the Q and A column on many occasions and pointed others to it as well.

The realization that this collection should appear all together in one book came when I was reviewing all of our past issues and was amazed at the diversity of topics that had been covered, each with painstaking accuracy and effort on the behalf of Dr. Rakocy.

Covering 10 years of questions posed and answers provided, *Aquaponics Q and A* chronicles the developments in aquaponics as well as the growing base of applications, methods and crop choices. Dr. Rakocy presents the information in a user-friendly manner while sharing his vast knowledge of aquaponics from both a scientific and practical point of view.

The book is organized with the questions and answers grouped by topic and it includes all new photos to illustrate various points and subjects.

I am happy to state that collaborating on this book is just one of many efforts in which John Pade and I have had the privilege of working with Dr. Rakocy. Dr. Rakocy currently serves on the Board of Advisors and consulting staff for Nelson and Pade, Inc. He is co-teaching some of our workshops, providing input on system designs and client projects and will oversee new research in aquaponics through our company.

But, most importantly, over the years our shared passion for aquaponics has brought John, Jim and I beyond business associates, beyond collaborating on projects and beyond talking just aquaponics. We've become friends with similar interests; each believing aquaponics has the potential to change the face of agriculture around the world. And, oddly enough, a few years ago we discovered that we have had some very unusual coincidences in our lives besides all growing up in Wisconsin, loving fish and aquaponics. From a sacred tree on a beach in Thailand to a sea plane crash just off of St. Croix, we are connected through common friends, a doomed sailboat, circumstance and fate. But I'll save the details of this real-life story for another book.

I do hope you enjoy the *Aquaponics Q and A* book and the wealth of information it provides on aquaponics. When the idea for the Aquaponics Journal was conceived, the intention was to share information on aquaponics to provide a platform for aquaponics to grow into an industry. This book is a great contribution to that effort.

System Design and Components

> ## Raft vs. other methods for small-scale system

Question

I've been looking into doing aquaponics on a small scale and have been studying different designs. It seems the most common I've read about are the raft system like you use at UVI and the gravel-filled grow bed (S&S) type system. Can you tell me the advantages or disadvantages of each of these for a beginner?

Answer

There are advantages and disadvantages to both systems.

1.) An advantage of the raft system is its size flexibility. Lined hydroponic tanks for raft culture can be constructed to any size using block, concrete or metal walls and plastic liners.

Commercial tanks can be as large as 30 ft wide by 400 ft long (9.1 m x 121.9 m) or greater. The S&S system uses pea gravel in polyethylene tanks that are 8 ft (2.4 m) by 4 ft (1.2 m). The weight of the gravel requires that the tank be sturdy. To my knowledge, larger tanks have not been used.

2) There is much less infrastructure required to distribute water in a raft system. Water enters and exits the hydroponic tank through a single PVC pipe. As it flows through the tank it is mixed by aeration. The S&S system uses a lattice arrangement of PVC pipes over the entire surface area of the gravel to distribute

Leafy crops grown on in raft aquaponics

the water and solids evenly. A key concern is solids, which are not removed from the S&S system. If all the water entered the hydroponic tank at one point, the gravel would clog.

3) At least 35% of the feed input to an aquaponic system becomes solid waste. The majority of the solid waste from raft systems is removed by using settling tanks and filters. There is always a danger that solids will clog the gravel in the S&S system. As a result, solid loading must be light, which limits the feed added to the system and fish production.

4) Pea gravel is an excellent substrate for growing plants and has more versatility than the polystyrene sheets and net pots that are used to support plants in raft systems.

5) Gravel protects plant roots, whereas roots in raft aquaponic systems are exposed and susceptible to damage caused by zooplankton, tadpoles, snails or fish. If tilapia gain access to a raft hydroponic tank, they will quickly eat all the roots, which will stunt plant growth.

6) Gravels containing calcium carbonate dissolve in response

to the acids produced in aquaponic systems and, therefore, buffer the system. Raft systems require frequent pH monitoring and base addition for buffering.

➤ Hobby system setup

Question

I have a small home hydroponic system that consists of 4-6 ft (1.8 m) Nutrient Film Technique (NFT) gullies with 40 plants, mostly leaf veggies. I also have an old 55 gal (208 L) aquarium sitting around and I was thinking about giving aquaponics a try but first I have a few questions:

> *➤ Is this an OK ratio of tank volume to number of plants?*
> *➤ Do I need to add any additional filtration to the tank? I have a canister filter that can take any type of medium but I'm not sure if it will remove elements that could be beneficial to the plants.*
> *➤ Do I need anything on the bottom of the tank such as gravel to collect solids that drop from the water?*

Answer

The volume of your tank is not as important as the amount of feed you add to your system daily. That will determine how many nutrients are generated. Volume is of secondary importance though in determining nutrient concentration. In a raft system, as a guide, we feed 2 oz of fish feed/10.8 ft^2 (57g/m^2) of plant growing area/day. However, in a raft system we have 1 ft (0.3 m) of water under the raft. In an NFT system, there is less than 1/2 inch of water in the channels. If you used the same feeding ratio, nutrients could accumulate to toxic levels (greater than 2,000 ppm). Although I do not know the exact rate, which depends on the solids removal system and type of leafy vegetable, you would want to feed at a much lower rate.

Basil grown in NFT (nutrient film technique)

As far as additional filtration, you should add a solids removal component. The canister filter will probably clog quickly even with coarse media. Since your system is so small, I would add another small tank and fill it with orchard netting. When solid accumulation becomes too high, drain the tank and clean the orchard netting. You will probably need to clean it every couple weeks. It is not good to be too efficient in removing solids, because they will decay and release inorganic nutrients that are beneficial to your plants. However, too many solids consume large amounts of dissolved oxygen and produce ammonia as they decay. Ammonia is toxic to fish. I would not add gravel to the bottom of the fish rearing tank. You want it clear so that solids will move easily to a drain, pump or siphon tube for removal.

➤ Water flow rates; fish tank volume

Question

How do you calculate the water flow rate of a raft system? Is it based on the fish tank size or something else? I learned from your paper on aquaponics that your flow rates are about 100 gal (379 L)/min, divided proportionally among your tanks, but I want to build a much smaller system.

Answer

The total water volume of the four fish rearing tanks in the UVI commercial-scale aquaponic system is 8,240 gal (31,192 L). With a total flow rate of 100 gal/min (378 L/min), the retention time of the water in the fish tanks averages 82 min. We adjust the flow so that the tank with the largest fish nearing harvest size has a higher portion of the water flow and a retention time of 60 min or less while the tank with the smallest fish has a much lower portion of the flow and a retention time of 120 min or more.

Let's say that you want the total water volume in the fish rearing tanks to be 2,000 gal (7,571 L). Divide 2,000 gal by 82 min and you will get a total flow requirement of 24 gal/min. This total flow can then be apportioned between four fish rearing tanks as in the UVI system. However, if you design your system to have only one fish rearing tank, the design retention time in that tank should be 60 min. Therefore, if you have just one 2,000-gal rearing tank, the flow rate should be 2,000 gal divided by 60 min or 33 gal/min.

➤ Size of the water pump

Question

I have a 400 gal (1,514 l) tank and a 10 ft x 12 ft (3.05 m x 3.66 m) greenhouse and I want to use bream for my fish. I want to go with a 12volt DC motor on my pump. My questions are: How big of a pump should I use? What type is the best?

Answer

As a rule of thumb, water retention time in the fish rearing tank should be approximately 1 hour. A water flow rate of 6.7 gal (25.4 l) per min is required for your 400 gal (1,514 l) tank. Flow rate is calculated by dividing the tank volume (400 gal) by 60 min. I searched online for 12 volt DC water pumps and found a well known brand (Little Giant) that will pump 360 gal (1363 l) per hour. It costs less than $90. This flow rate will give you a 1.1 hour retention time, which is close enough.

➢ Degassing tank

Question

In your UVI system you have a degassing tank, apart from increasing the dissolved oxygen level for your grow beds, what are the other reasons for having this tank and is it necessary when you have air-stones through out your grow bed.

Answer

The degassing tank has several functions. The most important function is to remove gases produced in the filter tanks. As solids collect on the orchard netting in the filter tank, anaerobic zones (without oxygen) form. Chemical reactions, mediated by bacteria, occur in the anaerobic zones to produce nitrogen, hydrogen sulfide and methane gases. Decomposition of organic matter in the filter tank produces amounts of carbon dioxide gas. These gases should not be allowed to accumulate in the system. Hydrogen sulfide is toxic and carbon dioxide interferes with oxygen uptake by the fish. Heavy aeration in the degassing tank vents these gases to the atmosphere. Before a degassing tank was used in the development

Dr. Rakocy pointing out the aeration in the degassing tanks at UVI

of the UVI system, the first few rows of plants near the inlet of the hydroponic tank did not grow well.

Another purpose for the degassing tank is to provide a location for the capture of tilapia fry in the event that breeding occurs in the fish rearing tanks or clarifiers. There are deep, fine-meshed nets positioned under the two inlets to the degassing tank. These nets capture fry and prevent them from being carried into the hydroponic tanks where they would eat plant roots and significantly decrease production. The nets are removed and cleaned every morning and replaced with a set of dry nets. Another set of nets should be installed at the inlet to the hydroponic tanks for safety in case the degassing tank nets fail. For example, a small undetectable hole could develop in a fold of the net and allow fry to pass through. All the nets should be inspected regularly. Additionally, the degassing tank serves as a location for an internal standpipe well. There are three standpipes in the degassing tank that divide the water flow among the three sets of hydroponic tanks.

➢ Degassing tank, solids removal

Question
I've heard that the degassing tank in a UVI system is used to adjust nutrient concentrations for various crops. Please tell me how this works. Also, I've read that you remove the solid fish waste in your system. Why do you have to do this and what do you do with the solids that are removed from the system?

Answer
The degassing tank is not used to adjust nutrient concentrations. It is used to remove gasses (carbon dioxide, nitrogen gas, methane and hydrogen sulfide) and regulate the water flow to the three sets of two hydroponic tanks. In the degassing tank are three standpipes that have rubber collars. Water flows into the degassing tank at a rate of 100 gpm (379 lpm). The rubber collars are set at the same level so that discharged water is divided into three flows of approximately 33 gpm (125 lpm) each.

The solids removal component helps to regulate nutrient levels. In the UVI system, solids from the fish rearing tanks have to be removed before the water enters the hydroponic tanks. If the solids are allowed to enter the raft hydroponic tanks, they will cover the roots, create anaerobic (no oxygen) zones and kill the plants. The first stage of solids removal occurs when fish tank effluent flows through a clarifier where large solid particles settle out and collect in the bottom of a cone. Solids are drained from the clarifier three times daily.

The second stage in the solids removal process consists of two tanks containing orchard netting, which filters out fine solids that have passed through the clarifier. The filter tanks do play an important role in nutrient regulation, especially in regards to nitrate control. Nitrogen is the predominant nutrient in fish effluent. The nitrification process converts toxic ammonia, which is excreted from the fish, into nitrate, which is relatively non-toxic. Nitrate concentrations can become very high, which is good for the growth of leafy green vegetables. However, high nitrate levels decrease production in fruiting plants because they stimulate vegetative growth and inhibit fruit set. If large quantities of solids are allowed to accumulate in the filter tanks, anaerobic zones will develop and denitrifying bacteria will remove nitrate by converting it into nitrogen gas. Denitrifying bacteria grow in the absence of oxygen. If the filter tank is cleaned twice a week, anaerobic zones will not develop and nitrate levels will increase, which is good for leafy green vegetables. If the filter tank is cleaned only once a week, anaerobic zones will develop and nitrate levels will decrease, which is good for fruiting plants. In summary, the frequency of cleaning the filter tanks regulates the nitrate concentration.

The filter tank also plays an important role in increasing the levels of all nutrients in the system. While solids are held in the filter tanks between cleanings, bacteria break down the organic matter and release inorganic nutrients, which can then be absorbed by plants through their roots. This process is called mineralization. Solids are removed slowly from the system so there is time for mineralization to occur.

We collect the solids that are discharged from the aquaponic system in two small lined ponds that are continuously aerated. After the solids are decomposed by bacteria and stabilized, we pump the pond water onto the campus lawn, where it irrigates and fertilizers the grass.

➢ Depth of the raft tank

Question

What is the reasoning behind the depth you've chosen in the hydroponic component of your raft aquaponic system? To me, 18 inches (0.46 m) seems deep.

Answer

The hydroponic tanks are actually 16 inches (0.41 m) deep. The first large hydroponic tanks we built at the University of the Virgin Islands were constructed with two tiers of concrete blocks (a concrete block is 8 inches (0.2 m) high) with a liner inside.

Rafts tanks have 16 inch (0.41 m) depth at UVI

Later we used poured concrete walls with a liner, but we stuck with the 16 inches (0.41 m) height because it worked so well. In the hydroponic tank the water is 12 inches (0.31 m) deep and there is 4 inches (0.1 m) freeboard (tank space above the water line).

Since our systems are outside, this freeboard offers two advantages. It is a mini-windbreak for delicate transplants, although a larger windbreak is required if the wind is strong. During heavy rains, the hydroponic tanks will collect up to 4 inches (0.1 m) in rainwater (6,000 gal (22,712 L) in our commercial-scale system) which is a real advantage in our dry conditions.

There are small air stones (3 inches x 1 inch x 1 inch) every 4 ft in our hydroponic tanks. Air stones provide oxygen and mix the water. Influent dissolved oxygen (DO) concentrations, which average approximately 4 mg/L, increase to about 7 mg/L by the end of the 200-ft flow through each set of two hydroponic tanks. High DO levels promote good root development and plant growth and enhance the growth and activity of bacteria, which treat the water by oxidizing (removing) ammonia and nitrite, toxic waste metabolites.

The transfer of oxygen from air bubbles to water depends on several factors, one of which is depth at which air bubbles enter the water. Oxygen transfer efficiency increases with increasing water depth. A depth of 12 inches is marginal for efficient oxygen transfer from air. If the water depth decreased, diffused aeration [the process where diffusers (air stones) are used] would not be effective. The mixing caused by the stream of air bubbles increases exposure of roots to oxygen and nutrients and the exposure of bacteria to oxygen and waste metabolites.

Another reason for having 12 inches of water is that some plants such as tomatoes and okra have excessive root growth and their roots occupy the entire space.

➢ Polystyrene plant rafts

Question

My class and I are working on an aquaponics project. We have a 1,000 gal fish tank which we intend to raise tilapia in. Our assignment is to find a way to do this without polluting our environment, so we decided to raise basil in an aquaponics environment. Our problem is this: We may use the floating Styrofoam sheet method, but how exactly would we go about getting the nutrients from the fish water up to the roots of the plant? We have heard of the wick system, but could you please explain this a bit to us and help us out? Any assistance you can give would be greatly appreciated.

Answer

You should use sheets of closed cell polystyrene that float on the water surface of the hydroponic tank. Paint the surface of the

Plants growing on a raft made of dense polystyrene

20

sheets with a potable grade of white latex paint. This protects the polystyrene from sunlight, which would otherwise quickly deteriorate it. Drill 2 inch holes in the sheets. For basil we have used a spacing of 8 inches (20.3 cm) between plants in rows and 12 inches (30.5 cm) between rows. Use 2 inch net pots to support your transplanted seedlings. The net pots are 2 inch across at the top and 2 inch deep. There is a lip at the top that rests on the polystyrene and prevents the net pot from falling through. The net pot extends ½ inch (1.27 cm) into the water. When the transplant is placed into the net pot it touches water, which moves upward through capillary attraction, keeping the potting media moist. Very quickly the plant roots grow through the webbing in the net pot and extend deep into the water.

➢ Growing media for plants in rafts

Question

I am trying to grow herbs on my fish tank at school. I am floating some foam but I need some media to put my seedlings in. Do you have any suggestions? I wanted to use materials we have at school instead of ordering rock wool.

Answer

By foam I assume you are referring to floating sheets of Styrofoam. Actually, a better material is polystyrene. The cells in polystyrene are closed and it is stronger and more durable than Styrofoam. Dow blue board is made from polystyrene. It is normally used for building insulation but makes an excellent floating hydroponic support.

At UVI we buy polystyrene that is 1.5 inches (3.8 cm) thick. I also suggest that you paint the surface with a potable grade of latex white paint because sunlight degrades styrofoam and polystyrene very quickly. If you are using a raft system, then you should support your plants with 2 inch net pots which are readily available from hydroponics suppliers. Drill 2 inch holes in the polystyrene and insert the net pots which are supported by a lip around the top perimeter. Net pots also come in larger sizes. I'm not sure what you would have around your school as a starting media.

Maybe you could use sawdust or fine wood shavings as long as they do not come from treated wood which is toxic. You could also order standard media other than rockwool. You could use perlite, vermiculite, coconut fiber (coir) or a combination of these. I do not recommend using plant-starting media containing peat because peat can contain Pythium spores, a root fungus that can kill plants or retard their growth. Once you have a good healthy seedling, you can insert it along with the starting media into the net pot (don't worry if some of the media falls into tank, it will merely accumulate as a thin, harmless layer on the bottom) or you can gently wash off the media, being careful to avoid any root damage and place the transplant into the net pot. A mass of root will quickly grow through the spaces in the net pot and support the plant.

➢ Polystyrene is food safe

Question

I've noticed that raft systems use polystyrene for the rafts. Most of the polystyrene I've encountered either reeks of plasticizers or when older is brittle. Can plasticizers leach from the polystyrene into the water - and hence into the fish - in these systems? Is there a type of polystyrene that is best for use in these systems?

Answer

The expanded polystyrene used in aquaponics does not contain plasticizers, which are known as phthalates. Polystyrene is made from a long chain hydrocarbon with every other carbon connected to a phenyl group. There are some health concerns about workers who are exposed to high levels of styrene used in the manufacture polystyrenes, but the final product is widely used for food packaging and considered safe. The main concern of polystyrene is environmental because it is not easily recyclable and requires 900 years to decompose in the environment.

Phthalates are industrial compounds known technically as dialkyl or alkyl aryl esters of 1,2-benzenedicarboxylic acid. They are found in a variety of polyvinyl chloride-based products. Uses of phthalates include softeners of plastics, oily substances in perfumes, additives to hairsprays, lubricants and wood finishers. That new car smell, which becomes especially pungent after the car has been sitting in the sun for a few hours, is partly the pungent odor of phthalates volatilizing from a hot plastic dashboard. In the cool of the evening they condense to form an oily coating on the inside of the windshield. There are concerns about the effect of low levels of phthalates on the human reproductive system, especially in males. There is no cause for alarm in using polystyrene in aquaponic systems. However, I urge that polystyrene sheets be used carefully to avoid breakage, ensure long use and minimize environmental impacts.

➢ Drilling holes in the polystyrene rafts

Question

I'd like to know, what is the most practical and fastest way to drill the holes in the polystyrene sheets?

Answer

We make a template in a piece of $3/8^{th}$ inch plywood. Holes of the desired size are cut in the template in the desired pattern

with a 1 and 7/8th inch hole drill for 2 inch net pots or a Rotozip®
with a spiral drill bit for 3 inch net pots. The template is placed
over the polystyrene sheet, and holes are easily cut using the
template as a guide and the hole saw or Rotozip®. The template
and polystyrene sheets are both 8 ft long by 4 ft wide.

We use three templates with 1 and 7/8th inch holes for lettuce
production. An 88-hole template in a diamond pattern with 7 inch
(17.8 cm) centers is used for Bibb lettuce. We use either 60 or 48-
hole templates for red or green leaf lettuce. The 60-hole template
consists of 10 rows (across the width) with 9.6 inches (24.4 cm)
between rows. Each row contains 6 holes with a spacing of 8
inches between holes. The 48-hole template consists of 8 rows
with 12 inches between them. Each row contains 6 holes with 8
inch (20.3 cm) spacing. The 48-hole template produces larger
plants and is also used for sweet basil.

Every vegetable has a recommended spacing for optimum
production. Consult hydroponic books for information on spacing.
If you want to produce a plant that is not commonly raised in
hydroponic systems, obtain spacing recommendations for field
production and select the highest density.

> ## ➢ NFT (nutrient film technique) channels

Question
*I am considering using Schedule 20 3 inch (7.62 cm) pipe to
construct an NFT aquaponic system. I am a rookie and wondering
if the root structure will have problems supporting the plants. I'd
like to grow lettuce, herbs, flowers and possibly tomatoes. How
deep should I keep the water in the pipes?*

Answer
I suggest you buy NFT troughs, which are designed

specifically for hydroponic plant production. The trough bottoms are flat, which allows the roots to spread out. There is also a small recess in the bottom that gives additional space to the roots. The troughs are angled so that water flows quickly and evenly through them as a film less than 1/8 inch deep. The water distributes nutrients to all the roots and provides oxygen. Removable plastic covers fit over the troughs. There are openings in the covers for the plants to grow through, but the remainder of the trough is covered to prevent algal growth. The covers can be removed to easily clean the troughs in preparation for the next production cycle.

PVC pipes on the other hand are less than desirable. They are heavier and harder to work with. Plant roots cannot spread out and therefore accumulate in masses that can become thick enough to block the water flow, which creates anaerobic conditions and root death. PVC pipes are more difficult to clean.

It is my philosophy to always invest a little more at the beginning of a project which makes a recurring operation, such as pipe cleaning, simpler and faster. In the long run you will save money and get better results.

➢ Aeration and air diffusers

Question

I understand that the fish tanks and the raft tanks need to be aerated to provide enough oxygen in the water. What is the best way to achieve this? What is better: lots of small bubbles or fewer large bubbles? The aquaculture companies sell different sized air stones that provide different volumes of air. How do I determine the best size for a system? Also, I noticed you have a ring of air stones in your fish tanks. What is the reason behind this?

Answer

Oxygen exchange is based on surface area. Theoretically, it is better to have a large number of small bubbles than a small number of large bubbles. With more small bubbles there is more surface area, given the same amount of air.

The air stones we use in the UVI system are 6 in. x 1.5 in. x 1.5 in. (15.24 cm x 3.81 cm x 3.81 cm) and are designed to handle 0.5 ft^3 (0.03 m^3) of air per min. But, if you throttle back the air flow to get the small bubbles, I believe you are pushing substantially less air through the air stone and getting overall less surface area and oxygen exchange.

Aeration in the fish tanks provides adequate levels of dissolved oxygen at KP Simply Fresh, North Freedom, WI

We probably have more surface air with a lot of medium sized bubbles than fewer small sized bubbles. If you throttle back on aeration to get small bubbles, you are minimizing water circulation and you are not bringing up oxygen deficient deep water to the surface of the tank where a considerable oxygen exchange occurs with the atmosphere. We adjust aeration so that there is a nice swarm of bubbles at the surface that actually raises the surface of the water by a fraction of an inch.

We have 22 - 6 inch (15.24 cm) air stones per tank. However, with a 1-hp blower for 88 air stones we were not getting enough air. Therefore we increased the blower to 1.5 hp. We have one valve at each tank regulating the 22 air stones for that tank, and we keep that valve wide open.

In an aquaponic system with the high levels of dissolved organic matter, air stones clog quickly and the ability to get small bubbles does not last long. We clean our air stones once a week.

We put the air stones around the outside so that the food will concentrate in the middle of the tank. This prevents the fish from splashing out the food during the feeding frenzy. We used to have vertical lift pumps in the middle. The food therefore concentrated around the edge of the tank and a large amount of it wound up on the ground. The manifold floats and keeps the air stones at the same depth in all tanks regardless of water level. This is important because if the water in one tank got higher due to the drain clogging, then less air would go into that tank. However, right now we are resting the air stones on the bottom of the tank and no drain clogging occurs.

➤ Drum filter vs. orchard netting

Question
I have two questions specific to the design of the UVI aquaponic system. First, I have a question about preventing the growth of gelatinous material on the plant roots. I read that you leave some fine solid waste in system long enough to prevent the

buildup of gelatinous material on the plant roots. Can you explain how this works and why the fine solid waste trapped in the bird netting prevents the buildup of gelatinous material?

Secondly, did you ever use a drum filter followed by the orchard netting. My reasons for asking this are because: 1) Some people already have a good drum filter plumbed into the system. 2) A drum filter is easy to install and is a familiar piece of equipment to someone already into recirculating aquaculture. 3) I have found some good drum filters that are auto cleaning and use very little water to do their cleaning cycle.

Answer

Most of our engineering design breakthroughs are serendipity. When we switched to the drum filter, the problem with the gelatinous material occurred. When we switched back to orchard netting, the gelatinous growth went away. I believe the bacteria growing in the orchard netting absorb the dissolved organic matter or some portion of it so that there is no food for gelatinous bacteria to grow after that stage.

Adding a drum filter before the orchard netting tank is worth a test. I think the orchard netting would have to be cleaned very infrequently because no visible solids come through the drum filter. It would take a while for bacterial growth to develop on the orchard netting. I think this would work because the filamentous bacteria just need a holdfast which would now to be provided by the orchard netting. Good idea.

➤ Baffles in the clarifier

Question

Can you please give me the design info on the baffles in the clarifier in the UVI system? For instance, do they attach to the bottom of the cone shaped tank? Are they in a specific location for a reason and, if so, where are they located? Does the incoming water cause a swirling motion or is there a baffle that directs the incoming water in any direction? Would a water-jet near the tank bottom, which could be turned on during solids removal, aid in getting the water swirling to help the solids go down the drain? Could this water jet replace the swimming action of the fish you keep in your clarifier?

Answer

The center baffle goes down the full length of the cylinder. We use PVC sheeting to make it. We fix it in place with strips of 4 inch (10.16 cm) fiberglass down the side of the tank between the baffle and the cylinder. The baffle divides the cylinder into two equal halves. The inlets from the fish rearing tanks, one from each tank, immediately have a 45 degree coupling so that the water flows upwards, produces an upwelling current on the surface, but then flows downward as a plug flow which goes under the baffle in the cone portion. The solids settle to the bottom and the water flows upward.

A second shallow (approximately 12 inch (30.5 cm) baffle is located in front of the outlet parallel to the first central baffle. This second baffle helps keep floating solids from going through the outlet. We keep a few small tilapia fingerlings in the clarifier, and they work wonders. Besides dislodging solids from the cone and getting them to settle compactly at the bottom where they are easily removed, the fish swim down the 4 inch (10.16 cm) drain pipe to the plastic sock in the rearing tank. They keep the drain lines from constricting with filamentous bacteria. Without the fish, we had to clean the drain lines every day. With fish in the clarifier we never have to clean the drain lines. We just replace the fish every 3-4 months as they grow. The water jet idea may work partially, but I believe a lot of solids would settle back on the side of the cone when you turn off the jet.

Start-Up

> ## Quick start up?

Question

I am looking for a way to start an aquaponic system quickly. I understand the concept that you should stock each tank separately and stagger the stocking so you have regular harvests of fish. But, that means that it is months before you have enough nutrients to grow plants. How can you get going sooner? Is there any fertilizer, like aquatic plant fertilizer or hydroponic plant fertilizer, that you can add to get going that won't hurt the small fish?

Answer

As an aquaponic purist, I cringe at the thought of using inorganic nutrients in an aquaponic system with the exception of calcium, potassium and iron, which are not found at adequate levels in fish feed. That said, adding a hydroponic nutrient formulation would not affect fish that grow well in aquaponic systems. Eliminate any ammonia compounds from the formulation because fish generate enough ammonia from the outset and establishment of the biofilter for removal of ammonia requires 4 weeks, a time during which feeding should be restricted.

You would be surprised how quickly nutrients accumulate to levels that promote rapid plant growth. Using a 6 week stocking interval, the system will be fully stocked in 18 weeks. If you can delay planting by 4 weeks, there should be enough nutrient accumulation for good plant growth. If you do use a hydroponic formulation, I suggest a one-time addition at one fourth strength. If the pH and alkalinity of your source water are high, it may take a

31

long time for the pH to decline to a point where calcium hydroxide and potassium hydroxide additions are needed to maintain pH at 7. If calcium and potassium concentrations are low in the source water, deficiencies of these nutrients may occur in plants during the startup phase. In this case, you may have to supplement with soluble inorganic compounds such as calcium nitrate or potassium phosphate.

➤ Inoculating the system with bacteria

Question

I have read that you should inoculate your grow bed with nitrite-converting bacteria before getting started. If one does not do this, will the right bacteria grow naturally over time, given you have fish and plants in place already? Do you think the inoculation is necessary?

Answer

We never inoculate our aquaponic systems. Nitrifying bacteria occur naturally and large populations will become established in response to the buildup initially of ammonia and then nitrite. The establishment period is about one month, during which time you should use a very low feeding rate and monitor ammonia-nitrogen and nitrite-nitrogen levels regularly. If ammonia-nitrogen concentrations increase to 5 ppm (mg/liter), stop feeding until it starts to decrease. The same rule applies to nitrite-nitrogen, but nitrite is more toxic. Stop feeding if nitrite-nitrogen exceeds 2 ppm (mg/liter). Even this level of nitrite-nitrogen is high but chloride ions, which come from fish feed, reduce nitrite toxicity.

The acclimation period can be risky. One way to avoid this risk is to pre-condition the system by operating it for a month without plants and fish while adding ammonia to the system. Maintain ammonia-nitrogen concentrations at 10-20 ppm (mg/liter) for two weeks by adding an ammonia cleaning solution. You will also need to add some nutrients such as phosphorus fertilizer, trace elements and a base (maintain pH at 7.0-7.5 by adding calcium hydroxide and potassium hydroxide) to promote bacterial growth. In this situation it would be helpful to inoculate the system with bacteria because it will not be exposed to bacteria from plants and fish. Just adding some garden soil or pond bottom sediment to the fish tank should be sufficient. At the end of a month, exchange all the water, add fish and plants and begin feeding cautiously. I suggest that you initially monitor ammonia and nitrite closely, but you should be able to increase the feeding rate quickly while maintaining low ammonia-nitrogen and nitrite-nitrogen concentrations.

➤ Establishing bacteria

Question
I would like to know more about the bacteria in the system. Is it necessary to add a "starter bacteria" to get going or does it grow naturally when the system is in operation.

Answer
The bacteria that remove ammonia from an aquaponic system are called nitrifying bacteria. Ammonia is a toxic waste product that is excreted by fish. Ammonia is removed from the water by bacteria belonging to the genus Nitrosomonas, which derive energy through the oxidation of ammonia to nitrite. Similarly, bacteria belonging to the genus Nitrobacter oxidize toxic nitrite to relatively nontoxic nitrate. Nitrifying bacteria occur naturally and

do not have to be added to the system. However, these bacteria grow slowly in response first to the buildup of ammonia and then to the buildup of nitrite. Approximately one month is required before an active population of nitrifying bacteria becomes established. During this period, the feeding rate should be low and ammonia and nitrite concentrations should be monitored. If ammonia-nitrogen or nitrite-nitrogen concentrations exceed 5 and 2 ppm (mg/liter), respectively, feeding should stop until the concentrations decrease. If cultures of nitrifying bacteria are added to the system, the establishment period may be reduced. However, the cost of purchasing bacteria that exist naturally is generally not justified by a slight decrease in the establishment period.

➢ Determining system size for start-up

Question
I have been researching with the intent to build a moderate sized multi-family aquaponic system in southern Ohio. I sent for a few of the Aquaponics Journal back issue CDs so I can learn more. I do have two initial questions: In sizing a system, what kind of yields can be achieved? Is there an optimum system size with the best yields?

Answer
The ratio of fish feed/day/m^2 will ultimately determine yield. The desired feeding ratio ranges from 60 to 100 g/day/m^2. Every type of plant will have a different yield. At UVI we are working to determine yields of different plants. For example, we found that basil can produce 51.6 lb/10.77 ft^2/year (23.4 kg/m^2/year) while okra produces 29.5 lb/10.77 ft^2/year (13.4 kg/m^2/year). I think you may be referring to the total yield. Total yield of course depends on the size of the system. The UVI system has 2,303 ft^2 (214 m^2)

of plant growing area, so annual basil and okra production is 11,038 lb (5007 kg) and 6,322 lb (2,868 kg), respectively. Not only does basil obtain higher yields, but also it is at least 10 times more valuable than okra. The total yield that you want to achieve depends on the size of the system and the number of systems. You can obtain lower or higher total yields by making your system smaller or larger as long as you maintain a feeding ratio between 60-100 g/day/m2.

➤ Planning a system

Question

I am planning on setting up an aquaponic system and was wondering if you have any suggestions. I plan to construct a 15 ft x 33 ft (4.6 m x 10.06 m) PVC hoop house with 2-800 gal (3.03 m³) and 2- 500 gal (1.89 m³) tanks with 4 grow beds and several NFT channels. Water would flow by gravity from each tank to a grow bed, then to a sump to be pumped up to the NFT channels where it flows by gravity back to the tank again. I plan on setting the system up with hybrid bluegill and converting to walleyes once the bugs are worked out. I will use timed feeders for feed training then switch to demand type feeders. My biggest questions are where to put heaters and pH monitors in the system and whether it will be necessary to add an aerator. Also, will I need to buffer the system with potassium bicarbonate once it is up and running? The primary goal is fish production with veggies for home use secondary. I think I will need to keep the water temp below 72° (22.2° C) in the summer and above 60° F (15.5° C) in the winter. Winter crops may include broccoli, peas, lettuce, spinach and day-neutral strawberries. Summer crops may include tomatoes, cucumbers, peppers, beans and more strawberries. Please give me any feedback on my proposed design and crop choices.

Answer

Your crop choices seem fine considering that you will maintain fairly low temperatures which are preferred by vegetables. Bluegills should grow well but walleyes may be a challenge. We use red ear sunfish (shellcrackers) in our hydroponic tanks to control snails and they grow and multiply without feeding but the densities are low. The description of your system does not mention a solids removal component. It is important to remove solid waste before the water flows to your hydroponic component. I would put the heating system in the sump where it will not interfere with your fish rearing tanks or hydroponic tanks.

We place a base addition tank next to the sump and direct a small stream of water through it to the sump. When base is needed to maintain pH 7.0 to 7.5, we add a fixed amount of base to the base addition tank. It dissolves and slowly mixes into the system without creating peak values which may stress the fish. This system is very simple and does not require any automation. The need for base is variable but it is certainly not required more than once a day and it only takes a few minutes for manual addition. Potassium bicarbonate is not as cost effective as potassium hydroxide or calcium hydroxide. You will definitely need to add an aerator to your fish rearing tanks. We also aerate our raft hydroponic tanks. We use one 3 inch (7.62 cm) airstone every 4 feet (1.21 m). We have tried timed feeders (belt feeders) and demand feeders but they have ways of failing so now we prefer manual feeding. This allows us to observe the feeding response of the fish and make adjustments. Good luck with your operation.

➢ Adding plants, testing water quality

Question

I'm a girl who is a student at Liverpool High School and I am involved in a Research Class in which I am conducting an experiment on Aquaponics. I have been working on this project since last year and I was wondering if you could answer a few questions for me. I have fish in my system now; I put them in the system in September. I was wondering how long to I have to wait before I can start planting some plants?

Also I have been doing a few chemical tests on the water to make sure it is safe. I have been checking the alkalinity, chloride, hardness of water, dissolved oxygen, nitrite, nitrate, ammonia, and pH. Are there any other tests I might need to do? I have also been weighing the fish weekly.

Answer

It is usually a good idea to have the fish in the system for about a month before plants are added. During this period, a low feeding rate is required while bacteria become established in the biofilter, but some nutrients will accumulate.

When seedlings are planted in the system, nutrient levels will be adequate for their initial needs. After the month-long establishment period, the feeding rate can be increased considerably, which will cause a substantial increase in nutrient levels at the time that plants enter a phase of rapid growth.

Most of the water quality variables you listed are important for fish production management, but I would not be concerned with chloride or hardness. Sodium chloride is added to fish feed, and it could negatively impact plant production if it becomes too high, but this is generally not a problem in aquaponic systems. Hardness is a measure of the concentration of calcium and magnesium. It would be better to measure calcium and magnesium directly, but this is expensive and not necessary if you are using a good feeding rate ratio. Nitrate levels are primarily important in relation to plant production. It does not have to be measured very often, perhaps once a month. Dissolved oxygen, ammonia and nitrite should be measured frequently during system establishment. After that period, measuring these parameters once every two weeks is sufficient. As feeding rates and fish biomass increase, knowing dissolved oxygen (DO) levels becomes more important. You should maintain the DO concentration at 5 ppm (mg/liter) or higher. pH should be measured almost daily and maintained at 7.0 by adding base (calcium hydroxide and potassium hydroxide). We never weigh our fish during a production cycle. It stresses them, which could result in a disease outbreak, and could injury them, causing death of the injured fish. If you want to document fish growth rate, collect, weigh and count a small sample of fish every month.

System Management

> ### Sequential rearing of fish

Question

I am currently living in Taipei Taiwan and am setting up a small Aquaponics system. I will be setting up a system in a small greenhouse. I have chosen Taiwanese Tilapia either black or red and have a question regarding the amount of fish I should grow. What happens when the fish grow larger? If I start a system with ½ inch fish and they grow in the system do I have to remove fish as they get larger? Or, should I start the system with a combination of larger and smaller fish which could be harvested and make room for the smaller fish to grow?

Answer

I am going to use some quotes from a fact sheet that Dr. Masser, Dr. Losordo and I wrote for the Southern Regional Aquaculture Center (SRAC), #454: Recirculating Aquaculture Tank Production Systems: Aquaponics-Integrating Fish and Plant Culture.

"To recover the high capital cost and operating expenses of aquaponic systems and earn a profit, both the fish rearing and the hydroponic vegetable components must be operated continuously near maximum production capacity. The maximum biomass of fish a system can support without restricting fish growth is called the critical standing crop.

Operating a system near its critical standing crop uses space

39

efficiently, maximizes production and reduces variation in the daily feed input to the system, an important factor in sizing the hydroponic component.

If you have just one fish rearing tank as your question seems to imply, you will need to use a fish rearing method known as sequential rearing."

"Sequential rearing involves the culture of several age groups (multiple cohorts) of fish in the same rearing tank. When one age group reaches marketable size, it is selectively harvested with nets and a grading system, and an equal number of fingerlings are immediately restocked in the same tank. There are three problems with this system: 1) the periodic harvests stress the remaining fish and could trigger disease outbreaks; 2) stunted fish avoid capture and accumulate in the system, wasting space and feed; and 3) it is difficult to maintain accurate stock records over time, which leads to a high degree of management uncertainty and unpredictable harvests."

Despite these problems, sequential rearing is commonly used in commercial operations, and it should be used in smaller systems that employ only one fish rearing tank. Every month the largest fish should be harvested and an equal number of fingerlings should be stocked. Since tilapia require a 6 month growing period, there will be six size groups of fish in the rearing tank at any given time.

The challenge is to harvest the largest fish with minimal disturbance to the remaining population.

One of the better grading systems I have seen consists of a series of 1-inch PVC pipes tied together by three nylon ropes that go through holes located precisely in the same place at the top, middle and bottom of the PVC pipes cut to the same length. The pipes are separated by short, equal lengths of smaller PVC pipe through which the nylon rope is threaded, essentially creating a flexible PVC pipe grading system that can be used as a seine. The small spacer pipes should be adjusted to a length that will retain harvestable size fish (1.5 lbs (0.68 kg) as an example) and let the smaller fish swim through. Of course the ropes have to be tied tightly so that the distance between all the 1 inch pipes is equal. There can be no slack. As the grading seine is pulled through the tank, it must be flush against the walls and bottom of the tank so that fish cannot swim around it or under it. When all the large fish are retained in a small section of the tank, dip nets can be used to catch them.

Here is the citation for the fact sheet. It can be downloaded from the website of the Southern Regional Aquaculture Center: Rakocy, J.E., M.P. Masser and T.M. Losordo. 2006. Recirculating aquaculture tank production system: aquaponics – integrating fish and plant culture. Southern Regional Aquaculture Center, SRAC Publication No. 454, 16 pp.

> ## ➤ Staggered stocking of fish and plants

Question

I am looking for information on the staggering technique for production of tilapia and lettuce in the integrated aquaponic system. I read that this can increase the volume of both fish and plants grown in aquaponics. However, how do you start stocking fish in the system and how do you transplant lettuce at different stages?

Answer

Staggering production in an aquaponic system is definitely the best technique for fish and often, but not always, the best technique for plants. Using the UVI system as an example, we have four fish rearing tanks, one of which is harvested every 6 weeks. Total growing time for the fish in a given tank is 24 weeks but the overall system produces fish at 6 week intervals. By doing this you are applying feed (and nutrients to the plants) at a rate close to

Tilapia fingerlings ready to stock into the culture tanks

the design limit at all times. In the UVI system total daily feed application ranges from 40 lbs/day (18.1 kg/day) just after a tank is harvested to about 50 lbs/day (22.7 kg/day) just before the next harvest. There is nothing magical about four fish rearing tanks. You could have six tanks and harvest fish every 4 weeks. However, the plumbing may get a little more complicated. There are many possibilities depending on fish species, their growth cycle and market considerations. To start a staggered operation you must stock one tank initially and then wait a given interval to stock the second tank. The UVI system requires 18 weeks before it is fully stocked with fish.

As to the plants, the UVI system has had very good results staggering lettuce so that 25% of the lettuce is harvested weekly. Total production time for the lettuce is 4 weeks so lettuce is always in four stages of growth. By planting lettuce every week, 4 weeks are required before the system is in full production. But staggering may not work for other plants and may not work sometimes even for lettuce. The main drawback of plant staggering is insect or disease problems. For example, if you have a pest or disease problem and have only harvested a fraction of your crop, then you leave a reservoir of insects or disease organisms to infect the new crop. In this situation it may be best to harvest the entire crop and break the cycle, paying attention to sanitation so no inocculum remains to infect the next crop. Another reason against staggering is the difficulty of managing crops in several stages of growth. In these situations batch culture may be best. The system should be well established with regard to the fish so there is a large reservoir of nutrients for plant growth. Raft culture works particularly well in this regard because of the large water volume and large mass of nutrients.

Sometimes it may be necessary to rotate crops to circumvent insect and disease problems or to provide the best seasonal growing conditions for your crop. These techniques are always used in traditional agriculture. Although aquaponics is unique in many ways, it is not above some of the well proven principles of standard agricultural practices.

➢ Tilapia and vegetables in the same tank

Question

I am thinking about building an aquaponic system that combines deep-water hydroponics with raising tilapia. I'd like to know if the tilapia would eat the roots (mainly lettuce) even if they are well fed. Do you think that growing vegetables directly in the same pool you raise tilapia is possible?

Answer

Tilapia love to eat lettuce roots, or any other type of vegetable root for that matter, and will eat every root they can find. A drawback of raft culture is the possibility that tilapia may gain entry to the hydroponic tank. This is why we screen the aquaculture effluent before it enters the hydroponic tank. We use a very fine mesh that will capture tilapia fry and we clean the screen daily. If tilapia fry gain access to the hydroponic tank, they will grow quickly and eventually devour all the roots. The plants will not necessarily die but they become very stressed, especially during mid-day when transpiration is high and growth slows significantly. Roots still grow between the net pot and the side of the polystyrene raft. In fact the root mass becomes so thick in this protected area that it is very difficult to remove the net pot at harvest. You should never try to raise tilapia and vegetables in the same tank. If tilapia enter the hydroponic tank, the system will have to be stopped while the hydroponic tanks are drained and the tilapia are captured. Water drain lines connecting hydroponic tanks must also be pumped out and the drain lines must be washed with a caustic solution of calcium hydroxide to kill any tilapia that have hidden in them.

There are other reasons for not growing plants and tilapia together even if an effective screen barrier could be installed to separate fish from the plant roots. The rearing tank surface area should remain uncovered to observe the feeding activity of the fish and determine when to increase or decrease the daily feed ration. If you are using a blower and air stones for aeration, the water surface must be exposed to the atmosphere to promote gas exchange, i.e., the diffusion of oxygen into the culture water and the venting of carbon dioxide from the culture water into the atmosphere. Finally, solid waste in the rearing tank will adhere to the plant roots, reducing the uptake of nutrients and water and possibly killing the roots due to the formation of anaerobic zones.

There is a use for fish in the hydroponic tanks but not tilapia. We stock red ear sunfish in our raft hydroponic tanks to control snails and we have used tetras to control zooplankton. The stocking densities are very low and the fish are not fed formulated feeds. These fish do not interfere with plant roots.

➤ Suitable systems, irrigation time, filtration

Question

I am a student in Thailand at the Asian Institute of Technology and I am interested in doing a research study in aquaponics. Would you please help me with the following information?
- ➤ *Fruit, vegetables and leafy vegetables... which would be suitable for catfish effluents?*
- ➤ *What is the retention time of the irrigation water in the system?*
- ➤ *What are suitable systems... Drip, NFT or another culture?*
- ➤ *What type of clarifier/filtration systems would be suitable for removing solids from the catfish effluents?*

Answer

I know the Asian Institute of Technology very well. Two years ago I presented a seminar there on aquaponics. Recently I submitted a proposal with two AIT professors (Dr. Amrit Bart and Dr. Yang Yi) to do tilapia research in Thailand, Bangladesh, Nepal and Cambodia. I am pleased to see that aquaponic research has become an area of interest at AIT.

Basic to your question is the type of system you will be using to raise catfish. The standard method in Thailand is to use ponds, but nutrient concentrations in ponds do not generally reach levels that are sufficient for vegetable hydroponics. It may be possible to use the effluent from Clarias (walking catfish) ponds because these ponds are stocked and fed at exceedingly high rates. Clarias has an auxiliary breathing organ, which allows it to absorb oxygen from air, which is gulped at the pond surface. Therefore, poor water quality (low dissolved oxygen concentrations and high levels of organic matter and dissolved nutrients) is not a major consideration. In aquaponics fish are cultured in tanks, and the effluent from the fish rearing tanks goes through a solids removal component and a hydroponics component before it flows back to the rearing tanks for reuse. Since very little is known about Clarias pond effluents for aquaponics, I will base my answers on tank aquaponic systems and specifically on the UVI system.

A wide range of vegetables can be used. At UVI we have successfully raised lettuce, basil, mint, chives, collard, mustard greens, pak choi, tatsoi, dill, cilantro, recao, kang kong (Ipomea aquatica), tomatoes, okra, watermelons, cantaloupe, cucumbers, squash, bell peppers, hot peppers and pole beans. We have also raised two types of flowers (zinnias and marigolds) successfully. This list could be expanded, but we have not had time to test other crops. As long as the culture water has adequate levels of dissolved oxygen and nutrients and the temperature and pH is in the correct range, just about any fruit or vegetable can be raised hydroponically.

In our system the retention time of the fish effluent in the hydroponic component is 3 hours.

We prefer raft culture. It is easy to aerate the water with air stones. There is good mixing of the nutrient solution. There is adequate room for root growth and no possibility of clogging or stoppage of the water flow. If power fails, water remains in the hydroponic tank, and the plants are not stressed as in other systems. And the hydroponic tanks provide excellent biofiltration.

NFT systems can be used, but there is a danger that solids and excessive root growth can block the flow of water, leading to the formation of anaerobic zones (without oxygen), which will kill roots. All solids must be removed before water enters the troughs. I do not recommend drip systems because the emitters will clog with organic matter or biological growth.

We use a combination of clarifiers and filter tanks, containing orchard netting, to remove solids from our system. The clarifiers consist of cylindro-conical tanks in which the cone has a 45-degree slope. We stock male tilapia fingerlings in the clarifier to dislodge settleable solids that adhere to sides of the cone. We open an external standpipe (drain) three times daily to remove solids that accumulate at the bottom of the cone. The orchard netting in the filter tanks removes fine solids very effectively. Once a week the tanks are drained and the orchard netting is cleaned with a high-pressure water spray.

➤ Solids removal

Question

I'm planning to build an aquaponic system to raise fish and grow some vegetables for my family and, hopefully, have extra to sell at our local farmers market. Most likely, I'll raise lettuce and salad crops, plus I'd like to grow tomatoes, peppers and cucumbers. I like the idea of using all of the waste, like in the media bed system, but I notice that in the float system you use and show on your website, the solids are disposed of separately. What problems do you see with dumping the wastewater, solids and all, into a grow bed filled with media like perlite or gravel? Will the solids break down? Please provide input so I can build a system that will be productive and utilize the wastewater as a resource.

Answer

I have written often on the issue of solids. About 35% of fish feed will end up as solid waste. For example, if you give your fish 10 lbs (4.5 kg) of feed per day, they will excrete roughly 3.5 lbs (1.6 kg) of solid waste (measured as dry weight). Solid fish waste is very dilute. The sludge that we remove from our system at UVI on a daily basis is approximately 2% dry weight at best. Therefore, the wet weight of sludge will be 50 times heavier than the dry weight of solids in the sludge. The 3.5 lbs. (1.6 kg) of solid waste (dry weight) will be equivalent to 175 lbs. (79.4 kg) of wet sludge. That amount of sludge can overwhelm the treatment capacity (sludge will decompose over time) of an aggregate medium, such as perlite or gravel, and lead to the development of anaerobic conditions (no oxygen), which can cause water quality deterioration and harm or even kill your fish. There are successful

*Clarifier used for removing solids
in the UVI aquaponic system*

systems that let all the solid waste go to the aggregate hydroponic beds, usually consisting of pea gravel, but in these systems the fish stocking density and feeding rate must be reduced to a level that allows the hydroponic beds to treat the solids (allowing them to break down and stabilize like compost). In other words, the solids loading rate must be reduced. Less fish are produced in these systems compared to systems where most of the solids are removed. However, by not adding a solids removal component, construction costs are reduced, so there is a tradeoff.

At UVI we remove nearly all of the solids before the aquaculture effluent enters the raft hydroponic beds, but we remove the solids slowly to allow some decomposition of organic waste. Microbes break down the solids and release inorganic plant nutrients. By removing the solids we can produce more fish. Some operations remove all the solids quickly so even more fish can be produced relative to plants. There is nothing wrong with any of these approaches and the approach you adopt depends on your objectives. However, there is often a criticism in the aquaculture community that aquaponic systems are too heavily oriented towards plant production. To promote commercial development of aquaponic systems, I believe that fish production should be maximized.

➢ Establishing a fish hatchery

Question

Can you tell me what is involved in setting up and running a fish hatchery to supply fingerlings for an aquaponic system? It appears to be fairly easy to raise tilapia but, what equipment do I need to get the best results? Please give me an overview of the process you recommend from hatching to fingerling stage.

Answer

I'm going to answer your question by providing an excerpt from a fact sheet that I wrote for the Food and Agriculture Organization of the United Nations on Nile tilapia culture. Here is the link if you want to read the entire fact sheet: http://www.fao.org/fishery/culturedspecies/Oreochromis_niloticus

The fact sheet describes systems in ponds, cages and tanks. In the U.S., I recommend using hapas in aerated tanks for spawning and sex reversal and recirculating systems for advanced fingerling rearing. At UVI we use 3,000 gal aerated tanks with 8 ft by 8 ft (2.4 m x 2.4 m) hapas for spawning. After 5 days, we catch and examine each fish and remove eggs from the mouths of females where they are naturally incubated. Only a few females will spawn and carry eggs in a 5-day period. The eggs are transferred to a hatching jar for incubation. Using a small pump, water continually circulates between a 264 gal (1 m³) tank and the jar. As the eggs hatch and their yolk sac is absorbed, the fry swim to the top of the jar and are carried out by the current into a hapa suspended in the tank. When hatching is complete, the number of fry is estimated, and the fry are transferred to an empty hapa in another 3000-gal (11.36 m³) tank for sex reversal.

Excerpt from the above referenced fact sheet:

Seed supply

"Tilapia are asynchronous breeders. Hormones are not used to induce spawning, which occurs throughout the year in the tropics and during the warm season in the subtropics. Breeding is conducted in ponds, tanks or hapas (fine mesh net enclosures). The stocking ratio for females to males is 1-4:1 with 2 or 3:1 being the most common. The brood fish stocking rate is variable, ranging from 0.06 – 0.14 lbs/ft² (0.3-0.7 kg/m²) in small tanks to 0.04 – 0.06 lbs/ft² (0.2 – 0.3 kg/m²) in ponds. The popular hapa-in-pond spawning system in Southeast Asia uses 0.22 lb (100 g) brood fish stocked at 0.14 lbs/ft^2 (0.7 kg/m^2). Spawning ponds are generally 0.5 acres (2000 m^2) or smaller. In Southeast Asia, a common hapa size is 1,290 ft^2 (120 m^2). [At UVI we use hapas that are 8 ft by 8 ft by 4 ft deep (2.4 m x 1.2 m x 1.2 m).]

Brood fish are given high quality feed at 0.5-2 percent of body weight daily. Swim-up fry gather at the edge of a tank or pond and can be collected with fine-mesh nets. Fry collection can begin 10 to 15 days after stocking.

Multiple harvests (six times per day at 5 day intervals) are conducted up to a maximum of 8-10 weeks before pond drainage and a complete harvest is necessary. Tanks must be drained and recycled every 1-2 months because escaped fry are very predaceous on fry from subsequent spawns. Alternatively tanks or ponds are harvested completely after a 2-4 week spawning period. Production of optimum-sized 0.5 inch (<14 mm) fry ranges from 1.5 to 0.14 to 0.23 fry/ft^2/day (2.5 fry/m^2/day) or 9 to 27 fry/lb/day (20 to 60 fry/kg female/day).

In the SE Asian hapa method, fish are examined individually every 5 days to collect eggs. This system is much more productive, but it is labor intensive. Brood fish are more productive if they are separated by sex and rested after spawning.

Sex reversal

Commercial tilapia production generally requires the use of male monosex populations. Male tilapia grow approximately twice as fast as females. Therefore, mixed-sex populations develop a large size disparity among harvested fish, which affects marketability. Moreover, the presence of female tilapia leads to uncontrolled reproduction, excessive recruitment of fingerlings, competition for food, and stunting of the original stock, which may not reach marketable size. In mixed-sexed populations, the weight of recruits may constitute up to 70 percent of the total harvest weight. It is therefore necessary to reverse the sex of female fry. This is possible because tilapia do become sexually differentiated for several days after yolk sac absorption. If female tilapia receive a male sex hormone (17 α methyltestosterone, MT) in their feed, they will develop as phenotypic males. Fry collected from breeding facilities need to be graded through 0.13 inch (3.2 mm) mesh material to remove fish that are 0.5 inch (>14 mm), which are too old for successful sex reversal. Swim-up fry are generally 0.35 inch (<9 mm). MT is added to a powdered commercial feed or powdered fish meal, containing >40 percent protein, by dissolving it in 95-100 percent ethanol, which is mixed with the feed to create a concentration of 60 mg MT/kg feed after the alcohol has evaporated. The alcohol carrier is usually added at 200 ml/kg feed and mixed thoroughly until all the feed is moist. The moist feed is air dried out of direct sunlight, or stirred in a mixer until dried, and then stored under dark, dry conditions. Androgens break down when exposed to sunlight or high temperatures.

Fry are stocked at 280 to $372/ft^2$ (3000 to $4000/m^2$) in hapas or tanks with water exchange. Stocking densities as high as $1,860/ft^2$ ($20,000/m^2$) have been used if good water quality can be maintained. An initial feeding rate of 20-30 percent body weight per day is gradually decreased to 10-20 percent by the end of a 3 to 4 week sex-reversal period.

Rations are adjusted daily, and feed is administered four or more times per day. If sex-reversal is conducted in hapas, the feed must be of a consistency that allows it to float. Otherwise a considerable amount of feed would be lost as it settles through the bottom of the hapa. Sex-reversed fry reach an average of 0.2 g after 3 weeks and 0.4 g after 4 weeks. The average efficacy of sex-reversal ranges from 95 to 100 percent depending on the intensity of management. [*The instructions for making MT feed are directed at readers from other countries. It is illegal for an individual to make MT feed in the U.S. In the U.S., powdered feed containing MT can only be purchased from Rangen, Inc. in Buhl, Idaho. Rangen is participating in a project sanctioned by the Food and Drug Administration called Investigations in New Animal Drugs.*

This study is being administered by the Fish and Wildlife Service in Bozeman, Montana. An aquaculturist can purchase MT feed from Rangen if he or she registers with FWS, pays a fee and keeps meticulous records. This investigation is nearing completion, and it is expected that the restrictions on purchasing MT feed will soon be lifted. In the meantime it is much easier to purchase sex-reversed fingerlings from a hatchery.]

Nursery

After sex-reversal, fingerlings are generally nursed to an advanced size before they are stocked into growout facilities. This procedure increases survival in the growout stage and utilizes growing space more efficiently. Sex-reversed fingerlings are stocked at approximately 1.9-2.3 fish/ft^2 (20-25 fish/m²) in small ponds and cultured for 2-3 months to an average size of 1.06 – 1.41 oz (30-40 g). The ponds should be filled immediately before stocking to prevent the build-up of predaceous aquatic insects. Final biomass at harvest should not exceed 5,280 lbs/acre (6,000 kg/ha).

Fish hatchery at UVI

In ponds, fingerlings are given extruded feed (30 percent protein) at an initial rate of 8-15 percent of biomass per day, which is gradually decreased to a final rate of 4-9 percent per day. A series of small cages (<4 m³) with increasing mesh size can be used to rear advanced fingerlings. Sex-reversed fingerlings can be stocked at a rate of 3000 fish/m³ and grown for 6 weeks until they average 0.35 oz (10 g). Fish of this size can be restocked at 2500 fish/m³ to produce 0.88-1.6 oz (25-30 g) fingerlings in 4 weeks. These fish can be stocked at 1500 fish/m³ to produce 1.8 – 2.11 oz (50-60 g) fingerlings in 4 weeks. A recirculating system stocked at 1000 fish/m³ will produce 1.8 oz (50 g) fingerlings in 12 weeks. Fingerlings should be fed 3-4 times daily."

➢ Inputs to the UVI system: energy, water, fish food

Question

What are the typical inputs in the UVI aquaponic system? How much electricity, energy, water, fish food, etc, are used in a day? What volume of water is flushed out of the filter tanks every day?

Answer

We recently calculated energy use by using electric meters. Our system has both 120 and 220 volt service. According to our meters, we use an average of 87.8 kw/hr per day. Electrical rates vary considerably by location. If, for example, electrical rates in your area are 20 cents per kw/hr, electrical costs would be $17.56 per day.

Water use averages about 1.5% of system volume per day. About half of this water is lost by evaporation from the water, transpiration from the plants and splashing. The other half is lost through sludge removal. The system volume is 29,375 gal (111 m³). Therefore the daily water requirement averages 440 gal (1.66 m³). However, we now have technology, the Geotube®, where we can filter almost all of the water from the sludge and return it to the system, thereby reducing the daily water requirement to approximately 220 gal (0.83 m³). The average daily feeding rate is 47 lbs (21.3 kg). The range of daily feed input will be from 40 lbs to 54 lbs (18.1 – 24.5 kg) over a 6-week period.

➢ Water usage in the raft system

Question

What percentage of water loss do you experience over 30 days time period using the raft system? Is there a formula that you've worked out for usage per plant?

Answer

We have not worked out water loss formulas for different plants. There are so many factors to consider, such as wind speed, air temperature, solar radiation and relative humidity. We have an outdoor system in the tropics in a trade wind zone. Much more water would be consumed per plant in our system than in a system located in a greenhouse in a temperate region.

The UVI system is designed so that the water level of only one tank, a sump, will fluctuate due to water loss from evaporation, transpiration, splashing and sludge removal. As the water level decreases, a float opens a valve to add new water, which is recorded on a meter. We take daily water readings and record total water consumption. If water usage is exceptionally large one day, we check to see if there is a leak in the hydroponic tank liners or if plant roots, which were torn off during harvesting, clogged a screen and caused water to back up in the hydroponic tanks. The usual reason is the latter, and we simply clean the screen. If it rains, the water level can rise up to 4 inches (10.16 cm) (a total of 6,000 gal (22.7 m^3)) in the hydroponic tanks where it is stored. In that case, the system will not require new water for a couple weeks.

In a 3-year trial with leaf lettuce, an older model of the UVI system, which contained 24,200 gal (91.6 m^3) water, consumed an average of 370 gal (1.4 m^3) per day or 1.5% of the system volume. Leaf lettuce, planted at two densities (1.49 and 1.86 plants/ft^2), was grown on a total area of 2,304 ft^2. Water loss from sludge removal accounted for 24% of the water loss from the system. Splashing, evaporation and transpiration accounted for the remaining water loss. Water use was 30 gal/lb of total tilapia production. In addition, each 30 gal (0.11 m^3) of water produced approximately 5.7 heads of lettuce.

➢ Lettuce spacing and growth rates

Question

I am interested in growing lettuce using aquaponics. Is it possible to get any information from you regarding growth time frames and how far apart they should be grown etc?

Answer

There are three major types of lettuce: butter (Bibb) lettuce, leaf lettuce (red and green) and romaine lettuce. At UVI we grow the lettuce on polystyrene sheets that are 8 ft long x 4 ft wide (2.4 m x 1.2 m). Each sheet has an area of 32 ft^2 (3 m^2). For maximum growth I suggest a planting density on a per sheet basis of 88 plants for Bibb lettuce, 48 plants for leaf lettuce and 32 plants for romaine lettuce. We use diamond spacing with 7 inch (17.78 cm) centers for Bibb lettuce. For leaf lettuce we use eight rows crosswise with six plants per row.

Lettuce seedlings are planted at a distance of 12 inches (30.5 cm) between rows and 8 inches (20.3 cm) within rows. For romaine lettuce, which is the largest lettuce, I suggest using eight rows with four plants per row. The distance between rows and between plants within rows would be 12 inches (30.5 cm).

We grow lettuce transplants in a greenhouse for 3 weeks. The culture period in the aquaponic system is 3 weeks for Bibb lettuce, 4 weeks for leaf lettuce and 5 weeks for romaine lettuce. It is generally best to stagger lettuce production so that you can harvest a portion of the system's lettuce every week and therefore provide a consistent supply to your markets.

> ## Harvesting and restocking fish

Question

I've been studying your system design and have a question for you. If you have 4 tanks for fish, what happens to the water quality and nutrient availability for the plants when you harvest one tank. Do the plants suffer from the sudden change in biomass and feed input?

Answer

When one tank is harvested, it is immediately restocked that same day with 1.8 oz (50 g) fingerlings. There will be a large decrease in feed to that tank, but the feed added daily to the other three tanks in the system will not be affected. As a result, the daily feed applied to the entire system will fluctuate between a low of about 40 lbs (18 kg) after a harvest to a high of about 55 lbs (25 kg) just before a harvest. This feeding cycle occurs over a span of 6 weeks. The lower feed level is still sufficient to supply adequate nutrients to the plants. In addition, the water volume - 29,000 gal (110 m^3) of the system provides a large reservoir of nutrients.

With a water depth of 1 ft (30.5 cm) in the hydroponic tanks, we are generally unable to see a decrease in nutrient levels as water flows through each set of two hydroponic tanks, a total distance of 200 ft (61 m), in 3 hours. In fact, we have been able to stop the flow for 2 weeks to make system repairs without affecting plant growth.

➤ Nutrients, spacing and production levels

Question

On our farm near George in South Africa, we recently built a commercial aquaponic system with sharp-tooth catfish in the fish tank. We believe that ours is the first commercial aquaponic system in South Africa. We need to know the following if you will be so kind to give us information:

1. *What are the different nutrient values of the fish water? Our stocking density is $250kg/m^3$ and our water temperature is 78.8° F (26° C).*

2. *If we plant tomatoes and peppers, do we need to add additional nutrients for the plants?*

3. *In aquaponic systems, what should the plant and row width be (distances between plants) for tomatoes and peppers?*

4. *What is the potential harvest, under normal conditions, for tomatoes and peppers?*

Answer

Your stocking density is amazingly high. For aquaponic systems with diffused aeration, I recommend a final stocking density of 60 kg/m3. If pure oxygen is used for aeration, a final density of 120 kg/m3 is feasible. Higher densities reduce individual fish growth rate and require longer culture periods to reach marketable harvest sizes. There is also a greater risk of disease due to stress and feed use efficiency decreases, which leads to increased production costs.

To answer your remaining questions I have asked for the assistance of Dr. Nick Savidov, Research Scientist, at the Crop Diversification Center South in Alberta, Canada. He has been using the UVI aquaponic system to study the production of a number of vegetables, including tomatoes and peppers.

Dr. Savidov shares, "We did not find any special demands for nutrients when growing tomato and bell pepper crops. The principal is the same: iron is very important. The use of Fe-DPTA, an iron chelate, to supplement iron is the most economical method. Concentrations of 1 ppm (mg/liter) are sufficient for raft culture, but the use of up to 3 ppm (mg/liter)will not hurt and will provide some stability for continuous operations. Potassium will be important as we found it can be a limiting factor at pH 6.2. In short, iron and potassium will do the job.

An optimal density for tomato culture in greenhouse conditions is 3 plants/m^2 and for bell pepper it is 3.3 to 3.5 plants/m^2 with two

Cherry tomatoes grown in aquaponics

59

shoots per one root, considering the entire area of the greenhouse. On the raft surface area the density should be 4-6 plants/m^2 depending on light conditions. The distance between plants should be 13-15 inches (35-40 cm). There is no difference between aquaponics and hydroponics as light and maintenance will be the major determining factors. With artificial lights the density can be increased up to two times.

A target production for tomatoes is 50 kg/m^2 and for peppers it is 23-28 kg/m^2. These values are not easy to achieve, but it is possible as our experience has demonstrated. The major problem for raft culture of tomatoes and bell peppers is the development of a massive root system leading to anaerobic conditions in the inner part of the roots. These are ideal conditions for Pythium, a root fungus, to attack. The probability of the attack increases with the age of the plants. Therefore, it is not recommended to keep the plants more than 4-5 months."

➢ Adding nutrients for plant growth

Question

I am creating a small aquaponic display of peppers and gold fish for the museum floor. I am looking for information on what additional fertilizers I will need for aquaponic peppers that will also be safe for the fish.

Answer

If you are using a properly designed aquaponic system, you will get most of the required nutrients from the fish and their feed. If you are using hard source water which is high in calcium, potassium and iron, then no nutrient supplementation is required. However, be prepared to add calcium, potassium and iron because these nutrients are not supplied in sufficient quantities by fish feed. At the University of the Virgin Islands we use rainwater and must, therefore, supplement with calcium, potassium and iron. We use calcium hydroxide and potassium hydroxide to maintain pH in the range of 7.0-7.5. At the same time we are supplementing calcium and potassium. Every 3 weeks we add 2 ppm (mg/liter) of iron in a cheated form, an organic form that does not precipitate out of solution. An important design criterion that we follow is to feed the fish at a rate of 2 oz (57 g) per square meter of plant growing per day. This rate gives us sufficient nutrients for good plant growth. However, this rate was developed for a raft system and lettuce. If you are using a nutrient film technique with substantially less water, then the rate could be lowered. We haven't specifically developed an optimum rate for peppers but we have gown peppers successfully. Peppers seem to grow slower than lettuce, again indicating that a lower feeding rate could be used. As a general rule, try to supplement minimally or you will be defeating the purpose of aquaponics, which is to recycle nutrients from fish culture, thereby reducing nutrient discharge to the environment.

Water Quality

pH

> ## Maintaining pH

Question

What kind of pH can be expected with aquaponic systems and what controls are used if needed? I expect it to be similar to using organic fertilizers in hydroponic systems. Am I correct in assuming that once the bacterial field is established pH is maintained by the bacteria culture?

Answer

Actually the bacteria in an aquaponic system lower the pH and you must constantly monitor pH and add base (calcium hydroxide or potassium hydroxide) to raise the pH and maintain it near a value near 7.0. A major group of bacteria in an aquaponic system are called nitrifying bacteria. They first transform ammonia to nitrite and then transform nitrite to nitrate. This is a process that produces acid and destroys alkalinity, thereby lowering the pH. If you allow the pH to decrease to pH 6.0, as an example, the efficiency of the nitrification process decreases, and toxic ammonia and nitrite accumulate. You want to maintain ammonia-nitrogen and nitrite-nitrogen levels around 1 mg/liter. In our system we measure pH every day and add base several times a week.

➤ Managing fluctuations in pH

Question

One of the biggest issues we deal with on a daily basis is the maintenance of pH in our system. We have six independent units in our tilapia based aquaponic system so pH control and automation will be relatively expensive (at our current scale of operation). What we do now is add potassium bicarbonate to each system each and every day. This seems to keep the pH in check but doesn't do much for adding buffering capacity. The pH swings up and down fairly quickly. After we add our potassium bicarbonate the pH will rise from say 6.2 to 6.6 or 6.8 but will be back to 6.2 or lower the very next day. In aquaculture I am aware that sodium bicarbonate is a good buffering agent, but have been advised that this agent is not suitable for aquaponics as sodium will block or compete with nutrient uptake by the plants. Is this true?

Also, I recently read an article where pure plaster-'o-paris (from Home Depot^{TM}) 'pucks' were dropped into the fish tanks and slowly dissolved over time thereby assisting with pH control and buffering. All of the plaster-'o-paris available in Canada (including Home Depot^{TM}) has hardening agents added to it and makes it unsuitable for contact with food fish.

I am interested in knowing if there are recommended pH buffering/adjusting agents for aquaponic operations and if there are any recommended simple means to automate the application of these agents to the aquatic system. Thanks for any information you can give.

Answer

Aside from feeding and removing solid waste, the next biggest daily chore in operating an aquaponic system is maintaining the pH. Fish excrete waste nitrogen through their gills in the form of ammonia gas (NH_3), most of which is immediately converted to ammonium (NH$_4$). Nitrifying bacteria in the system oxidize the ammonium to nitrite (NO$_2$) and then to nitrate (NO$_3$). The hydrogen ions (acidity) produced by this process destroy alkalinity and pH declines. Decreasing pH is a good sign. It indicates that the biofiltration (nitrification) process is working. You should never allow pH to decrease below 7.0 because the efficiency of nitrification is reduced at lower pH values resulting in an increase in ammonia. Try to maintain pH in the range of 7.0-7.5. This may be counter to what plants prefer but it is necessary in an aquaponic system. You should not add sodium bicarbonate because high sodium levels in the presence of chloride are toxic to plants. There are several basic compounds that can be used to neutralize acid in an aquaponic system. At the University of the Virgin Islands we alternate between calcium hydroxide [Ca(OH)$_2$] and potassium hydroxide [KOH]. A molecule of calcium hydroxide has twice the neutralizing capacity as a molecule of potassium hydroxide or potassium bicarbonate [KHCO$_3$]. Using current prices and the atomic weight of these compounds, the following table shows the calcium hydroxide is the most cost effective base:

Compound	Atomic Wt.	Cost/lb ($)	Cost/lb *1 ($)
Ca(OH)$_2$	74	0.24	0.09
KHCO$_3$	100	0.82	0.82
KOH	56	1.30	0.72

*1 Footnote: Cost adjusted for equal neutralizing capacity using 1 lb. of KHCO$_3$ as the basis for comparison.

Potassium hydroxide is a little less expensive than potassium bicarbonate when neutralizing capacity is considered. Although the potassium compounds are more expensive than calcium hydroxide, they are used to supplement potassium, often leading to better plant production.

You are right about the automation of base addition. It would require a mixing tank, a chemical dosing pump, an electrode for continuous pH monitoring and computer controls. We use a hand-held pH tester and add a given weight of base daily determined by experience. We add the base to a small well aerated tank that receives a small flow of system water. The high pH water enters the system slowly over several hours and does not stress the fish or plants.

➢ pH of 6.2 - impact on fish and plants

Question
I am reading back issues of the Aquaponics Journal and one of them has a brief statement about Dr Nick Savidov and his studies in Canada. It mentions how he uses a pH of 6.2 in his system. Prior to reading this, all references I've read about pH in aquaponics say that it should be kept at 7.0. Please tell me more about how this affects the tilapia and plants. What are the pros and cons of running the pH at 6.2?

Answer
It is difficult to compare systems because there are so many variables. A pH of 6.2 is not optimal for nitrification; the bacterial-mediated transformation of toxic ammonia to toxic nitrite to relatively non-toxic nitrate. The optimum pH is in the range of 7.5 to 8.0. However, a pH of 6.2 is optimum for hydroponic plant production in part because the most of the nutrients required for plant production are more soluble and available for uptake by plants at this pH. It is my understanding from conversations with Dr. Savidov that the pH in his system remains stable at 6.2 and that there is no need to add base (i.e., alkalinity). Since nitrification destroys alkalinity and lowers pH, his system is counteracting the

reduction of pH by other mechanisms. The makeup water (water added daily to replace system water loss) could be highly alkaline. Rapidly growing plants secrete alkaline compounds through their roots. And if there are anaerobic (no oxygen) zones in the system in pockets of sludge, a process called denitrification (the transformation of nitrate ions to nitrogen gas) will occur. Denitrification produces (recovers) alkalinity, the alkalinity lost through nitrification. There are other variables too such as fish loading and feeding rates, the feeding rate ratio and the ratio of daily feed input to plant production area.

In Dr. Savidov's latest aquaponic system, organic solid waste is not removed from the system. It is collected in a heavily aerated compartment and allowed to decompose. The end product of bacterial decomposition is carbon dioxide and water plus the release of nutrients to their inorganic state, which become available for plant nutrition.

In the UVI system, most of the organic solid waste is removed from the system, and base (either calcium hydroxide or potassium hydroxide) must be added several times weekly to maintain a pH at 7.0. In the UVI system fish stocking and feeding rates are high, and therefore high rates of nitrification are necessary to remove ammonia and nitrite. The UVI system reaches a compromise between nitrification and nutrient availability by maintaining pH at 7.0. Both systems are used to grow tilapia which can tolerate a wide range of pH. It appears that in both systems there are sufficient nutrients for rapid plant growth. Without the addition of calcium hydroxide or potassium hydroxide bases in Dr. Savidov's system, I assume there are sufficient levels of calcium and potassium in the makeup water, which is probably hard well water. Fish feed alone does not generate sufficient levels of calcium and potassium for maximum plant growth. The UVI system uses rainwater, which is devoid of nutrients, and therefore calcium and potassium must be supplemented along with iron.

➤ pH and Alkalinity

Question

We have been operating a small aquaponic system for a couple years now. We want to add aquaponics to a 14,000 gal (53 m³) recirculating aquaculture system (R.A.S.) How can we maintain alkalinity without using sodium bicarbonate? We have used potassium & calcium hydroxide to maintain pH. If you could, please give us some ideas. I appreciate it.

Answer

I think you are referring to the normal practice of adding sodium bicarbonate as a base to recirculating aquaculture systems without plants. As I have mentioned in this column before, sodium is not good for plants and, therefore, aquaponic systems require other bases. I always recommend the alternate addition of equal amounts of calcium hydroxide and potassium hydroxide to maintain pH in a range of 7.0-7.5.

There are sophisticated ways of adding base by using continuous sensing pH probes, computers and automatic dosing equipment, but I prefer a simpler technique. Divert a small stream of water from the discharge pipe of your pump (we tap the pipe and install a ¾ inch PVC water line) to a small circular tank such as a plastic 55-gal (0.21 m³) barrel which we call the base addition tank. Use one air stone to vigorously aerate the water in the base addition tank. Have the effluent from the base addition tank enter a sump from which water is pumped to the fish-rearing tank or have the water enter the fish-rearing tank directly.

Monitor pH daily. When base is needed, add either calcium hydroxide or potassium hydroxide to the base addition tank. On average, we add 35.3 oz (1,000 g) of base per day to our 30,000-gal (113.6 m³) system but the base requirement is variable and some days none is needed. Water from the base addition tank will slowly enter the system and rapidly become diluted, thereby avoiding spikes (high levels) in pH that would harm the fish or the plants. Potassium hydroxide dissolves quickly while calcium hydroxide requires a much longer period to dissolve. However, water is constantly entering the base addition tank and being mixed by the air stone so that most of the calcium hydroxide gradually dissolves, although a small amount usually remains on the bottom of the tank. This method is simple and reliable and requires only a few minutes of your time per day.

> ## ➤ Low system water pH (6.0)

Question

Right now my system (one 125 gal (0.47 m³) poly fish tank and a 32 ft³ (.9 m³) grow bed) is running with an extremely low pH (6.0 or below) and I am beginning to have a gradual die-off of fish. Obviously, this concerns me. The city water I use for replenishing the system when needed is around 7.4 - 7.6 pH. Today I performed a water change of about 35 gal (.13 m³) and the pH has barely moved up to 6.0. I don't know if this might be contributing but my grow bed is filled with granite gravel that was donated by a local quarry.

My question is two-fold...1. Any idea what may be causing my pH to continue to be so low? And, 2: If I can find some oyster shell or limestone gravel to mix in with my gravel, would my system benefit from it? How much would I need to make a difference? Is there an easier way?

Answer

What happens in an aquaponic system is that fish excrete waste nitrogen in the form of ammonia gas through their gills. This gas

(NH_3), which is very toxic, is quickly transformed to ammonium ions (NH_4) which is not toxic. At low pH values like yours all of the ammonia is in the non-toxic ammonium form. At higher pH values more of the ammonia shifts to the toxic gaseous form. Fortunately, nitrifying bacteria oxidize toxic ammonia to nitrite (NO_2), which is also toxic, and then oxidize nitrite to nitrate (NO_3), which is not toxic. The process of nitrification destroys alkalinity and the pH steadily declines. Nitrification is most efficient at pH values of 7 or above. If you let your pH drop to 6.0 or lower, nitrification will practically stop and very high concentrations of ammonium ions will develop. If you add a large amount of base and the pH increases rapidly, there will be a sudden shift to gaseous ammonia and your fish will try to jump out of the tank because their gills are being burned and then they will all die which is not a pleasant experience for the fish culturist or the fish. Therefore it is extremely important that you maintain your pH in a range of 7.0-7.5. In this range nitrification is very efficient and the ammonia and nitrite concentrations should be less than 1.0 mg/liter. Your fish may be dying due to low pH but low pH alone doesn't affect a hardy fish like tilapia (you do not mention the species). Other fish are more sensitive. If you add city water from the tap, the chlorine in it can kill fish. You should age city water for a few days in an aerated container before adding it to your system. The chlorine will dissipate. There may be other reasons your fish are dying, too.

Granite is not a good buffer and I would suggest replacing it with gravel containing some calcium carbonate which will dissolve slowly and maintain good pH values. Smooth pea gravel (mined from river beds) is often used as a hydroponic media. If pea gravel does not provide enough buffering to maintain your pH at 7.0-7.5, then you can add small amounts of calcium hydroxide which in powder form will dissolve much more quickly than calcium carbonate. Another good base is potassium hydroxide which dissolves instantly and supplements potassium. In either case you must add these hydroxide bases to your system slowly in small amounts and ensure that they are well mixed so that you do not create "hot spots" where the pH is very high and harms both fish and plants.

➢ Low pH (5.5) in well water

Question

We have well water with very low pH (5.5). I have been running an aquaponic system for about 5 months now and struggle to keep the pH high enough. I am alternately adding calcium hydroxide one day and potassium hydroxide the next day. I can get it to about 6.5 by the end of the day, and then it drops back down to 6.0. My concern is that eventually I will have too much calcium and potassium for the plants. Is there anything else I can add to raise pH?

Answer

A rapid decrease in pH indicates that your biofilter is working efficiently. That is a good sign. In the UVI system we sometimes add base every day, but the pH does not decrease nearly as fast as in your system. The UVI system utilizes hydroponic rafts to serve as the biofilter. The optimum feeding rate ratio for raft culture ranges from 60 to100 g of fish feed/m^2/day. At this rate nutrient levels remain relatively stable, plants grow well and there is sufficient nitrification to remove toxic metabolic waste products (ammonia and nitrite). Nitrification is an acid producing process that destroys alkalinity and decreases pH. The maximum treatment capacity of aquaponic rafts is equivalent to 180 g of fish feed/m^2/day. If a higher fish stocking density is used and the fish can consume an amount of feed equivalent to the maximum treatment capacity, there would be a higher rate of nitrification and

71

the pH would decrease faster. This leads me to believe that your system is not balanced and that you should either add more plants or reduce the fish stocking rate. Using a different base is not the solution to your problem.

I suggest that you send a water sample to a laboratory to determine the concentrations of all the nutrients in your system. A county extension agent should be able to give you the address of a certified laboratory in your area. The concentrations of calcium and potassium in hydroponic nutrient formulations are quite high (over 200 ppm (mg/liter), but you could indeed experience a nutrient accumulation problem. When we started our aquaponic research program in experimental systems, the ratio of fish to hydroponic growing area was much too high, and nutrient accumulation became a program. The concentration of total dissolved solids, a measure of total nutrient content, increased from 100 ppm (mg/liter) to 2,000 ppm (mg/liter) (the initial concentration of a hydroponic solution) after applying 22 lbs (10 kg) of feed to a water volume of 364 gal (1 m^3). If we had continued to feed the fish, nutrients would have accumulated to toxic levels. To solve this problem we had to reduce the fish stocking rate substantially.

➢ Raising pH

Question

Please could you suggest how much calcium hydroxide to add to an aquaponics system to raise the pH from a level of around 6. The system is comprised of a 713 gal (2700 l) fish tank and 107 ft^2 (10 m^2) of grow beds. I had been using calcium carbonate quite successfully but am currently really struggling to get the pH up. This could be due to the weather warming up here in Australia and an increased rate of nitrification.

Answer

Calcium carbonate dissolves very slowly and cannot be relied on to maintain pH of the 7.0, the recommended pH for aquaponic systems. Calcium hydroxide dissolves much faster, but complete dissolution requires some time (days) and a system that ensures maximum exposure of the culture water to the surface area of the compound. We use a base addition tank in the UVI aquaponic system to gradually add high pH water to the system. If the calcium hydroxide was added directly to the fish tanks, there would momentarily be 'hot zones' of very high pH water that could burn the gills of fish if they swam through them. When calcium hydroxide is added to the base addition tank, some of it dissolves immediately, but most of the compound settles to the bottom of the tank. A small side stream flow from the water pump outlet delivers culture water to the base addition tank, which is thoroughly mixed by continuous aeration. The calcium hydroxide gradually dissolves. Occasionally we stir up the calcium hydroxide at the bottom of the tank with a short section of PVC pipe to create more contact with the water. The base addition tank effluent enters the sump, where it is greatly diluted (no pH spikes) and immediately pumped to the fish rearing tanks.

The practical way to determine how much calcium hydroxide to add is through trial and error. If the pH goes down rapidly, add more base until you can maintain pH 7.0. Try not to exceed pH 7.0 because some essential nutrients precipitate out of solution at higher pH levels. There will be some variation in the rate of pH decline, and you are right that at higher temperatures in the summer biological activity speeds up (including nitrification). You may need to add base every day. And remember that we alternate the addition of calcium hydroxide with potassium hydroxide to supplement the system with both calcium and potassium ions.

Let me give you an example of an extreme case we once experienced. We were raising tilapia fingerlings in small (10 ft (3.05 m) diameter) tanks using biofloc technology. We fed four times daily, aerated heavily and removed excess solids twice daily. The feeding rate and nitrification rate were so high in this tank that we had to add base after every feeding. A measurable decrease in pH occurred hourly. Aquaponic systems require base less often, never more than once a day.

Another situation we sometimes experience is that pH remains stable for weeks at a time and no base is required, which indicates that excessive denitrification is occurring in anaerobic zones somewhere in the system. The process of denitrification produces alkalinity and negates the need for base addition. When fruiting crops are raised, we increase denitrification in the filter tanks by cleaning them less often. Denitrification reduces nitrate levels and promotes fruiting. However, if denitrification is excessive, no base addition is required, which could lead to calcium and potassium deficiencies. In this case, clean the filter tanks more often and check for and remove any anaerobic sludge deposits in the hydroponic component. Your nose will guide you because anaerobic zones give off foul smelling gases.

➢ Lowering pH

Question

My pH is around 7.6 - 8.0. How do I lower it?

Answer

You lower pH by adding acid. There are several options but sulfuric, nitric or hydrochloric acid can be used. If your system is

74

a hydroponic system (no fish), then you will want to lower the pH to approximately 6.0. Adding acid can be very dangerous if you add too much. Low pH values can burn the plant roots or cause chemical reactions that make essential nutrients unavailable to the plants, leading to nutrient deficiency and related diseases. Therefore, you must determine the correct amount of acid to add to reach the target pH. Take a 1 liter sample of your system water and use a pipet to add acid a drop at a time until the desired pH is reached. Stir the water sample as this is being done. Then read the pipet to see how much acid was added. Let's say, for example, that 0.5 ml was added to a 1 liter sample to reach pH 6.0. If the total water volume of your system is 1,000 liters, then you need to add 500 ml of acid. Add the acid to your reservoir very gradually or else you will create a plume of water with very low pH. As this plume passes through your plants it can damage or kill them even though a system pH of 6.0 results once the water is thoroughly mixed. Be careful when you are working with acid. You can add acid to water but NEVER ADD WATER TO ACID, especially if you are working with concentrated acid. This will result in a violent reaction that may splatter you with acid. Wear safety goggles and have fresh water readily available in case you spill acid and need to wash it off (dilute it) very quickly to minimize damage (to yourself or your facility).

If your pH is too high (7.6-8.0) as you say, I assume you must be working with a hydroponic system where pH frequently increases. In aquaponic systems, the pH always decreases in response to nitrification which is the oxidation of ammonia and nitrite to nitrate, mediated by bacteria. In an aquaponic system, you must always add base to bring the pH up to 7.0, a point where the bacteria that remove toxic ammonia and nitrite are most efficient. If your initial pH in an aquaponic system is 7.6 to 8.0, it will soon decrease (within 4 weeks) as the nitrifying bacteria become established. Do not add acid but do feed at very low rates during this period to prevent ammonia and nitrite buildup. This is a very critical period when novices (and experts too) kill fish. Ignore the demands of the fish for more food. It is better to underfeed them for 4 weeks than to kill them due to ammonia or nitrite toxicity.

Dissolved Oxygen

➢ Dissolved oxygen levels

Question

How much dissolved oxygen is required for plant growth? Do the bacteria need the same amount of dissolved oxygen, or more? What is the ideal DO level in the raft tank? Some raft systems that I read about do not aerate the raft tanks, only the fish tanks. Is this a bad idea?

Answer

This is a good question. If aquaponic raft tanks are not aerated and dissolved oxygen levels decrease to levels less than 5 mg/liter, plant growth will be compromised. If the system is fed heavily and solids removal is inefficient, the biochemical oxygen demand (BOD) (the sum of all the oxygen consumed by organisms within the hydroponic tank) could be so high that the water will become anaerobic, which will cause death of the roots and plants. Even if solids removal is efficient, a considerable amount of dissolved organic matter enters the hydroponic tanks and exerts a high BOD. As for bacteria, dissolved oxygen levels should be at least 2 ppm (mg/liter).

To use un-aerated hydroponic tanks successfully, the system could be stocked and fed at lower rates (which means less production) or the water retention time in the hydroponics tank could be decreased so there is less time for the oxygen to be consumed (which requires either a higher water pumping rate or smaller hydroponic tanks) or the water temperature could be lowered (colder water holds more dissolved oxygen).

High oxygen levels in the hydroponic tanks promote maximum plant growth and water treatment (purification). I have seen raft hydroponic operations (no fish, just plants) inject liquid oxygen into a water distribution system under the rafts to create oxygen levels slightly above saturation (levels that are higher than that which occurs naturally). The saturation level of dissolved oxygen at 75°F (24° C) is 8.2 ppm (mg/liter).

The UVI system has a small air stone - 3 inches by 1 inch by 1 inch (7.62 cm x 2.54 cm x 2.54 cm) every 4 ft (1.22 m) in the hydroponic tanks. As water flows through a set of two 100 ft (30.5 m) hydroponic tanks in 3 hours, a total of 48 air stones increases dissolved oxygen from 4 ppm (mg/liter) (influent value) to 7 ppm (mg/liter) (effluent value). Furthermore, the current created by these air stones ensures good mixing of the nutrient solution among the thick tangles of plant roots and produces a pronounced film of nitrifying bacteria on the underside of the rafts above the upwelling currents caused by the air stones. I strongly recommend that deep channel hydroponic tanks be aerated.

Water Temperature

➢ Optimum water temperature

Question

What is the optimum water temperature in aquaponics if you are raising tilapia? What about other fish, like trout or yellow perch?

Answer

The optimum water temperature for raising tilapia is 85°F (29.5°C). The ideal temperature range for rainbow trout is 55-60°F (12.7–15.5°C) although they can be raised at a maximum temperature of 70°F (21.1°C). Yellow perch grow well in a temperature range of 70-75°F (21.1-23.8°C).

Vegetables generally account for the majority of income in an aquaponic system, and therefore it is important to satisfy the temperature preference of the vegetables over that of the fish. Most vegetables will grow well with water temperature in a range of 70-75°F (21.1-23.8°C), which coincides well with the temperature preference of yellow perch. For rainbow trout the system should be operated at a water temperature of 70°F (21.1°C) or slightly less.

An aquaponic system should be operated at less than optimum temperatures, 70-75°F (21.1-23.8°C) for tilapia, although tilapia will grow reasonably well and produce commercial levels in this temperature range. Of course I am assuming that the aquaponic system is set up in an environmentally controlled greenhouse. In outdoor systems in the tropics, such as the UVI system, temperature is dependent on climate. In the UVI system water temperature ranges from 73°F (22.7°C) in the winter to 84°F (28.9°C) in the summer.

Crops such as lettuce flourish in the winter but decline somewhat in the summer. In this case it is a good strategy to switch to heat tolerant vegetables such as cucumbers, cantaloupe, okra, etc. during the warmer months.

➢ Manipulating water temperature between fish and plants

Question

I am a senior at Baylor University. I'm doing research on aquaponics for third world applications and I have a question about water temperatures. From my reading I noticed that most, if not all, use the same temperature in the fish tank as in the plant growing beds. Has anyone tried to have the fish's water stay at 80-85°F (26.6-29.4°C) and then cool the water to 65-75°F (18.3-23.9°C) before it enters the growing beds? This could be a possible way to limit disease such as pythium as well as maximize production. If so, has anyone tried low tech designs such as subterranean cooling of the water and solar heating?

Also, I am doing a thesis on aquaponics and, specifically, the effects of cleaning frequency on the production of nitrates and phosphates. Do you know of any peer reviewed journals on aquaponics for my bibliography page?

Answer

It would be difficult and costly to involve both cooling and heating devices in one system because the retention time within components is relatively short. The commercial-scale UVI aquaponic system has a total water volume of 29,000 gal (110 m³), which is circulating through the system at a rate of 100 gal (0.38 m³) per min. In one 24-hour period, the culture water circulates through the system approximately five times. Five times the volume of the system is 145,000 gal (549 m³). Therefore, on a daily basis you would have to heat 145,000 gal of water and cool 145,000 gal of water. You could attempt to maintain dual temperatures by heating alone and letting the system cool naturally if you are in a cold climate or cooling alone and letting the system heat naturally if you are in a warm climate. Let me give you two examples.

At UVI we once experimented with cooling towers to decrease water temperatures in the hydroponic beds during summer. We built the towers at the influent end of the first hydroponic tank in our small experimental systems, which contained two hydroponic tanks, each measuring 20 ft by 4 ft by 16 inches (6.1 m x 1.2 m x 0.4 m). The cooling towers, consisting of corrugated plastic media, were 28 inches (0.71 m) long (direction of air flow) by 30 inches (0.76 m) wide by 36 inches (0.91 m) high. The media was enclosed in a wooden plenum (enclosure) on three sides. The media comprised the fourth side of the plenum. A poultry fan was mounted in the wooden wall opposite the media wall and blew large volumes of air through the media as culture water, distributed at the top of the cooling tower, trickled down through the media. Evaporation cooled the water. The cooled water flowed from the first hydroponic tank into the second hydroponic tank and from the second hydroponic tank into a sump. A water pump in the sump divided the return flow between the fish rearing tank and the cooling tower. This cooling system was turned on only at night. Daytime air temperatures were too high to achieve cooling. The cooling towers lowered the water temperature by only a few degrees Fahrenheit due to our high relative humidity, which hinders evaporation. Cooling towers would be more effective in climates with low relative humidity. We did observe that additional energy was required for the water pump (extra flow was needed to return water to the cooling tower) and fan, and a considerable amount of water was lost to evaporation. Cooling towers in our situation did not appear to be economically feasible.

In temperate regions, water needs to be heated in greenhouse-based aquaponic systems during winter. Heat exchangers are generally installed in the sump. Therefore the warmest water goes to the fish rearing tank. As water flows through the hydroponic tanks, it cools.

I am not aware of commercial applications of subterranean cooling and solar heating. Subterranean cooling has potential for cooling greenhouses in temperate climates during the summer. I'm from Milwaukee, and I remember how cold tap water was even during summer. In the tropics the earth is not that cold, and subterranean cooling would not be effective. Solar heating could be used as a supplemental heat source for aquaponic systems during winter in northern climates. However, wintertime solar radiation is generally low in northern climates and other heat sources would be needed.

John Hargreaves and I wrote a review paper on aquaponics in 1993 (see reference below). You will be able to find a number of journal citations in that paper. After 1993 the word "aquaponics" came into being. A database search of "aquaponics" or "aquaponic systems" should turn up more recent publications.

Rakocy, J.E. and J.A. Hargreaves. 1993. Integration of vegetable hydroponics with fish culture: a review. Pages 112-136 in J.K. Wang, editor. Proceedings of the Aquaculture Engineering Conference on Techniques for Modern Aquaculture. Aquacultural Engineering Group, American Society of Agricultural Engineers.

Other Water Quality Considerations

➢ Water quality monitoring

Question

I am planning to set up an aquaponic system with a 500 gal (1.9 m³)fish tank and an attached, gravel-filled grow bed. What test equipment for monitoring water quality do you recommend. Are meters available for everything I need to test for?

Answer

I take a minimalist approach on water quality monitoring. I prefer to design the system according to standard specifications and use the correct ratio of daily fish feed input to plant growing area. When the correct ratio is used, I find that very little water quality monitoring is needed. The S&S Aqua Farm in Missouri has designed the best-known gravel-based system. A volume ratio of 1 ft³ (0.03 m³) of tilapia rearing tank to 2 ft³ (0.06 m³) of hydroponic media (0.2-0.4 inch pea gravel) is recommended for a reciprocating (flood and drain) system. A 950 gal (3.6 m³) rearing tank with a final tilapia density of 0.5 lbs (227 g) of fish per gal of water is supported by eight hydroponic tanks that measure 8 ft x 4 ft x 1 ft deep (2.4 m x 1.2 m x 0.3 m). At the recommended ratio, no solids are removed from the system and no nutrient supplementation is necessary. However, some supplementation may be necessary if your water source does not have enough iron or potassium. The hydroponic tanks are stocked with red worms to help break down and assimilate organic matter. I assume the fish are fed to satiation two or more times daily.

I recommend that you be prepared to monitor dissolved oxygen, pH, ammonia and nitrite at the minimum. These parameters are primarily important in regards to fish health.

Dissolved oxygen should be maintained at 5 ppm (mg/liter) or higher. A pH of 7.0 is best for both fish and plants. Ammonia and nitrite should be in a range of 1 ppm (mg/liter) or less. If low dissolved oxygen is detected, additional aeration may be required or the feeding rate should be reduced. Pea gravel is usually a good buffer to the acids that are produced in the system and, therefore, the pH should be stable. During the start-up phase before nitrifying bacteria become established in the gravel biofilter, there is a danger of ammonia and nitrite reaching toxic levels. I recommend feeding very low rates during the first 4 to 6 weeks and monitoring ammonia and nitrite several times a week. When the biofilter is fully established with bacteria, it will not be necessary to monitor ammonia or nitrite regularly. An occasional check, perhaps monthly, is all that is necessary. Ammonia and nitrite will increase if too much organic matter accumulates in the biofilter or something (e.g., chlorinated water, antibiotics, neither of which should be used) kills the nitrifying bacteria.

You can purchase test kits for these parameters from aquaculture supply catalogs. I do not recommend meters because they would be too expensive for the scope of your operation. Test kits are inexpensive and consist of reagents that are added to a measured sample of water. A chemical reaction occurs in proportion to the concentration of the test parameter and produces a colored solution, which is compared to a color chart that indicates the approximate concentration of the parameter.

Plants require 13 nutrients in sufficient amounts for good growth. If a nutrient deficiency occurs, it is best to send a water sample to a commercial laboratory for analysis. The cost is reasonable. Many laboratories are also capable of analyzing leaf tissue samples for nutrient levels. The lab will compare the nutrient concentrations in the sample to a normal range of concentrations in healthy leaf tissue. A combination of these tests should identify the deficient nutrient or nutrients. In the UVI raft hydroponic system, calcium, potassium and iron are deficient and need to be supplemented. The system uses rainwater, which contains little or no nutrients. If your system uses well water, there may be sufficient amounts of iron and potassium. Also gravel will supply nutrients as it dissolves and neutralizes the buildup of acid in the system.

➢ Electrical conductivity and nutrient concentration

Question

I am an avid hydroponic grower and have been experimenting with aquaponics. I have a 200-gal (0.76 m³) tank where I am growing tilapia and I have a connected, perlite-filled grow-bed. So far, I've grown lettuce and basil and the plants have grown well. In hydroponics, I've always used an EC (electrical conductivity) meter to test the concentration of fertilizer (salts). When I check the EC of the water from the fish tank, the reading is minimal. For instance 400-600 micromohs, but the lettuce and basil are growing fine. I would need a reading of about 1500-1800 micromohs in hydroponics to grow these same crops. So, what is it I'm measuring in the aquaponics? If it is salts, as in hydroponics, where does it come from and why do the aquaponics plants do well with such a low EC? How can I measure the nutrients available to the plants in aquaponics?

Answer

This is a very good question that illustrates one of the major differences between hydroponics and aquaponics. Your conductivity meter is working just fine and you are measuring the same plant growth nutrients in aquaponics as you measure in hydroponics. What you are finding is that plants require less nutrients to grow well. I think that higher nutrient levels are recommended for hydroponics as a safeguard in the event that

84

plants go through a growth surge or the operator forgets to check the nutrient solution for a few days. The plants depend totally on the inorganic nutrients that are added to the hydroponic solution. In aquaponics, nutrients are being generated continuously. They are either excreted directly by the fish or they are being released in an inorganic form from the breakdown of organic matter. Even if the fish are not fed for a few days, there is a lot of organic matter in the system that continues to generate nutrients through a process called mineralization, the release of minerals through microbial decomposition.

Let me elaborate further by using total dissolved solids (TDS) as another measure of nutrient levels in hydroponic solutions, although TDS is not as accurate as EC. A typical nutrient solution has a TDS level of 2,000 ppm (mg/liter). As the solution is used, individual nutrients are extracted at variable rates by the plants. Depending on the volume of the solution relative to the plant growing area, the nutrients will become depleted or unbalanced in a matter of days or weeks. At this point the TDS level may be less than 500 ppm (mg/liter) as an example. Then either the solution is discarded entirely and a new solution is made or all the individual nutrients (plants require 13) are measured and new nutrients are added to bring them back to their original concentrations.

In our commercial-scale aquaponic system, TDS levels are seldom higher than 500 ppm (mg/liter), but they are being adjusted daily through natural processes to maintain this concentration which is adequate for good plant growth. Except for calcium, potassium and iron, the approximate correct balance of the other 10 nutrients is maintained. The levels of calcium, potassium and iron are not adequate in fish feed for good plant growth and these nutrients must be supplemented in most aquaponic systems. What we are concerned about in aquaponics is maintaining the correct ratio of daily feed input per unit of plant growing area to generate adequate amounts of nutrients for the plants. The optimum ratio depends on many factors (type of plant, batch vs. staggered production, etc.), but we generally recommend a feeding rate ratio of 60-100 g/day/m^2 of plant growing area.

Your EC readings of 400-600 micromohs are sufficient to lettuce and basil growth. If the EC levels decrease and plant growth declines, increase the feeding rate. If the fish cannot consume more feed, then you should increase the stocking rate.

➤ Adding salt for fish health

Question

I have been raising fish in aquariums for many years and I want to add a small aquaponic grow bed. I am thinking of building a media-filled bed that sits on top of a fish tank. I will pump the water from the fish tank into the bed and then let it drain back to the fish tank. The question I have is related to salt. In my aquariums, I always add pure salt (at a rate of 1 tbls/10 gal) to help keep my fish healthy. But, I read that salt is a problem for the plants. Is there a level where it is ok? Are some plants tolerant of higher salt levels?

Answer

I would eliminate the addition of salt if you are going to raise vegetables, although some vegetables and herbs like tomatoes, cucumbers, lettuce, mint and watercress are moderately tolerant to elevated salinity. However, yields decline as salinity increases. Feed manufacturers add small amounts of salt to feed for the reason you suggest, so adding more salt is not necessary and would be detrimental to the plants. Furthermore, in a closed recirculating system such as an aquaponic system, nutrients salts from the fish feed tend to accumulate because the water exchange rate is low. Most people think of salt as sodium chloride, but dissolved nutrients (ions) are also considered to be salts. Magnesium, calcium, potassium, nitrate, phosphate, sulfate and the trace elements are nutrient salts. The total quantity of nutrient salts can be measured and expressed as electrical conductivity (EC) or total dissolved solids (TDS). In our early work at the University of the Virgin Islands before we knew the correct feeding rate ratio, we stocked too many fish relative to the plant growing area and found that TDS concentrations reached 2,000 ppm (mg/liter) after feed input reached 10 kg/m^3 of culture water. Any additional increase in TDS could be toxic to the plants. High TDS levels reduces water uptake by plants.

The accumulation of sodium (Na) is a concern in aquaponic systems because high sodium levels in the presence of chloride (Cl) are toxic to plants. The maximum Na concentration should not exceed 50 ppm (mg/liter). High Na levels will interfere with the uptake of potassium and calcium. In lettuce, reduced Ca uptake leads to tip burn, resulting in an unmarketable plant. Reduced uptake of calcium in tomatoes causes blossom end rot.

Adding a small amount of salt to fish culture water reduces the physiological work a fish must do to eliminate excess water. Water naturally moves from low salt concentrations to high salt concentrations in an effort to equalize the concentrations, a process known as osmosis. The salt concentration is much higher in a freshwater fish than the surrounding water. Therefore water moves into the fish, and the fish must continually use energy to excrete excess water. By adding some salt to the culture water and increasing its salinity, there is less osmotic pressure, and the fish does not have to work as hard to eliminate excess water.

Question

I am an avid aquarist and am setting up an aquaponic system in a window in the south side of my house to grow vegetables. I have always added salt to my aquariums to improve fish health and help reduce stress and disease. I understand that the salt is not good for the vegetables. Can I add a little bit? How much salt can the plants take and how can I measure it?

Answer

I advise against adding sodium chloride. We never add sodium chloride to the UVI aquaponic system. The limit for hydroponic systems is said to be 50 ppm (mg/liter). That would be 0.07 oz (1.9 g) of salt in 10 gal (0.04 m³) of water. There usually is some sodium chloride in surface or well water. In addition, there is salt in fish feed, and nutrient salts other than sodium chloride will accumulate in your system and provide some benefit. Depending on the water exchange rate, total dissolved solids (consisting mainly of nutrient ions) will range from 500 to 1,000 ppm (mg/liter) or higher in your system. This is equivalent to 0.67 – 1.4 oz (18.9 - 37.8 g) of total dissolved solids in 10 gal (0.04 m³) of water. However, you could experiment if your system is small and you don't mind starting over if your experiment fails. As I stated in another answer, plants like tomatoes can tolerate higher levels of salt.

➤ Alkalinity

Question

I am an aquaculturist looking into aquaponics. In much of the documentation I've read of aquaponics, there is very little discussion of alkalinity. In aquaculture, this is a key factor. Can you tell me how low or high alkalinity affects an aquaponic system and what you use to adjust it?

Answer

Alkalinity is the measure of the ability of a solution to neutralize acid. Total alkalinity is measured by adding acid (titrating a known concentration of acid) into a water sample until all the alkalinity is consumed, which occurs at a pH of 4.5. Alkalinity is expressed as the weight of the number of molecules of calcium carbonate ($CaCO_3$) that are equivalent to the number of molecules of acid (hydrogen ions: H^+) used to reach pH 4.5.

A major breakdown product in the metabolism of fish is ammonia, which diffuses through its gills into the culture water. Ammonia is toxic and must be removed from the water. In aquaponic systems as in recirculating systems in general, ammonia is removed through a process called nitrification. Ammonia is oxidized to nitrite, another toxic metabolic product, which in turn is oxidized to nitrate, which is relatively non-toxic. As soon as ammonia (NH_3), a gas, contacts the culture water, most of it is transformed to an ammonium (NH_4^+) ion, which is not toxic. Acid (H^+) is produced as NH_4^+ is transformed to nitrite (NO_2^-) first and then to nitrate (NO_3^-). This acid destroys alkalinity and pH decreases as a result.

It is very important to maintain pH at 7.0 by regularly adding bases (alkaline compounds) to the system. If bases are not added, the pH will decline to 4.5 and all the alkalinity will be consumed. As pH declines to 6.0 and lower, nitrification slows and eventually ceases, and ammonium concentrations, which usually remain around 1.0 mg/liter, will increase to 100 ppm (mg/liter) or higher. If the aquaculturist discovers that he or she has allowed the pH to decrease to a very low level and adds a large amount of base to quickly raise the pH, a large portion of the ammonium will be instantly converted to toxic ammonia gas. All the fish will react by explosively jumping out of the water, as the ammonia is burning their gills, and then quickly die. If very low pH is discovered, it should be brought up very gradually over many days with small base additions until nitrification resumes and removes the excess ammonium.

In the UVI system we monitor pH daily and alternately add calcium hydroxide base [$Ca(OH)_2$] or potassium hydroxide base (KOH). The system has a volume of 29,000 gal (110 m^3) and a daily feeding rate of 40 to 50 lbs (18-22.6 kg). We generally add 35.3 oz (1000 g) of either $Ca(OH)_2$ or KOH to the base addition tank. The frequency of base addition varies from daily to once a week or more depending on the pH. We are mainly concerned with the pH and not the concentration of alkalinity, which averages approximately 50 ppm (mg/liter) as $CaCO_3$.

The periods during which the pH is stable and base additions are not required may in part be due to denitrification, the process whereby nitrate ions are converted to nitrogen gas (N_2) by anaerobic bacteria, bacteria that require the absence of oxygen. Denitrification recovers/produces the alkalinity that was lost in the nitrification process. Anaerobic conditions develop in the organic matter that accumulates in the filter tank. Cleaning the filter tank more frequently, twice a week, will decrease denitrification. Denitrification may also occur in the organic debris that gradually accumulates at the bottom of the hydroponic tanks. We recommend that the hydroponic tanks be cleaned once a year.

Plants nitrate uptake and physiology also affects pH levels. In aquaponic and hydroponic solutions the majority of nitrogen exists as nitrate ions. As plants absorb nitrate ions they must reduce them to ammonium ions before they can be utilized for growth. In the process alkalinity is produced and bases are excreted from the plant roots, thereby raising pH. In hydroponic systems acid must be added to lower pH. In aquaponic systems the acid produced by nitrification generally exceeds the amount of base produced by plants. However, when optimum growing conditions occur and plants are at their maximum stage of growth, base excreted by plants may neutralize the acid produced nitrification, thereby stabilizing pH and negating the need to add base.

It is probably a combination of denitrification, nitrate physiology and other factors that work together to eliminate the need for base addition for long periods. This is not good because base addition in needed to supplement calcium and potassium, which are generally deficient in aquaponic systems. Removing anaerobic zones in the filter tanks and the bottom of the hydroponic tanks restarts pH decline and the need for base addition. There is nothing that can be done about nitrate physiology other than staggering plant production so that all the plants are not in their maximum growth stage at the same time.

➢ Algae growing in system

Question

I live in Florida and have recently set up a backyard aquaponic system. I have two 500 gal (1.9 m³) fish tanks, connected to shallow plant beds that are filled with Leca Stone (expanded clay pebbles). I flood the beds with the water from the fish tank several times a day.

The tilapia are growing and my seedlings seem to be doing pretty well. But, after two months, there is algae growing in the fish tank and on the surface of the plant beds. Everything is getting pretty green. Is it ok to have algae growing in an aquaponic system? Do I need to get rid of it? If so, how do I do that?

Answer

Nutrients that go into the production of algae are nutrients that are lost to the production of your cash crop. Algae can contribute to the clogging of the growing bed, which prevents even distribution of water and nutrients among plant roots. If the algae die, oxygen will be consumed as cells decay, and toxic ammonia and nitrite will be generated. Finally, some algae produce off-flavor compounds, which affect fish quality, or they may produce compounds that interfere with beneficial organisms in the system. Therefore, it is best to avoid the growth of algae. Eliminating algae from an aquaponic system is easy. Simply do not allow sunlight to make direct contact with the water, which is accomplished by shading all the water surfaces. Some sort of opaque canopy should be constructed over open water surfaces such as the rearing tank, sump and solids settling tank. Canopies can be constructed at a height of 7 ft (2.1 m) so that access to tanks is not hindered. As for the growing bed, add the culture water below the surface and do not allow the water to reach the bed surface before it is returned to the system. At UVI we created a water distribution system in the past by establishing a compartment under the media (expanded clay pebbles in your case) and supporting the media on a screen, usually vinyl covered hardware cloth. Water is then added from the bottom, flows up through the bed but does not reach the media surface before it is discharged back into the system through a bottom drain.

➢ Algae in a flood-and-drain system

Question

I have a small aquaponic system in my backyard in Florida with some tilapia and vegetables (lettuce, tomatoes, squash, beans and peas). The fish tank is not sheltered from the sun and there is a lot of algae growing in the fish tank and now in the gravel-filled grow bed. The water is basically green and getting thick. Do I need to get rid of the algae? How do I do it?

Answer

Yes, you need to eliminate the algae. We do not allow algae to grow in the UVI aquaponic system. Nutrients in an aquaponic system should be used for the production of vegetables and other plant crops rather than algae, which has no commercial value. We prevent algae from growing by using an opaque plastic sheet to shade the fish rearing and solids removal tanks. A Quonset structure supports the plastic sheet and provides space to work under the canopy. The hydroponic tanks are covered by floating polystyrene rafts, which shield the culture water from sunlight.

Plants are supported by net pots, which are inserted into small holes in the raft and secured by the net pot rim. The roots grow into the water below the rafts.

The surface of the gravel bed should be kept dry to prevent algal growth. A system called "ebb and flow" or "flood and drain" is generally used with gravel. The gravel bed is flooded intermittently below the surface to provide water and nutrients to the plant roots. When the gravel bed drains, air enters the bed and provides oxygen to the roots. The best way to achieve subsurface flooding is by creating a false bottom consisting of vinyl-covered wire mesh supported by a lattice of PVC pipes. The mesh must be small enough to retain the gavel. The false bottom provides a large area for water to rise into the gravel and drain from the gravel. The use of PVC drain pipes with holes to deliver and/or drain water from gravel beds is not recommended because the solid waste in aquaponic systems will clog the holes and render the pipes useless. If the beds cannot drain completely, anaerobic zones will form, killing the roots.

➢ Rainwater catchment

Question

We live in Portland, Oregon and are interested in raising tilapia in an outdoor aquaculture/aquaponic system. Is it possible to use rainwater collected off of my asphalt composition roof as the water for the tank? Will it be necessary to clean or purify the water prior to use? We are planning to create a biofilter/ aquaponic planting bed for the system. How do we size the filter and what do you recommend for the medium?

Answer

I would not use rainwater collected off asphalt roofing material for aquaponics. There is a possibility it will contain harmful compounds. If you collect rainwater, the catchment's surface should consist of material or a coating that is certified as potable grade, meaning that the water collected from this surface could be safely consumed by humans. There are paints or epoxy coatings, which are certified as potable grade, that could be applied to the asphalt roof. You will need to consult with a knowledgeable person at the paint store and obtain verification from the product label.

I recommend setting up an aquaponic system based on the technology developed at the University of the Virgin Islands (UVI). The UVI system employs raft culture, which consists of floating sheets of polystyrene. The plants are supported by net pots, and their roots grow freely into the water, not restricted by any substrate. Refer to previous issues of Aquaponic Journal for a detailed description. In the UVI system, the raft hydroponic subsystem is the biofilter. It provides enough surface area for the growth of nitrifying bacteria in combination with nutrient uptake by the plants to purify the water. In fact, the hydroponic sub-system has excess wastewater treatment capacity at the optimum feeding rate ratio for plant production.

The optimum feeding rate ratio varies from approximately 60 to 100 g/m^2 of plant growing area/day. The fish population needs to be manipulated so that most days the feeding rate falls within the optimum range. At UVI we use four fish rearing tanks per system. Fish production is staggered so that the fish are in four stages of growth. Each tank receives a different amount of feed, but the overall feeding rate to the system generally falls within the optimum range. If there is only one fish rearing tank, the optimum feeding rate could be maintained by raising fish of various sizes together. Each month the largest fish could be removed, and an equal number of new fingerlings could be stocked, resulting in an overall feeding rate that is fairly constant and within the optimum range. However, this method requires considerable fish handling, which is stressful to the fish.

Fish to Plant Ratios

> ## ➤ How many plants for 11,000 m² fish tank

Question

I have a few questions that I cannot find the answers to. Please tell me what is the ratio of fish to water in a system that holds 2,905,893 gal (11,000 m³) of water? How much fish do you need for so and so many square meters of plants? Does it vary based on what plants you have? How does the amount of fish food affect the plants or is that never a problem?

Answer

A system that is *2,905,893 gal* (11,000 m³) is huge. That system would occupy 12.5 acres (5 hectares) and that is not a workable size for an aquaponic system. Perhaps you mean 29,059 gal (110 m³). That is the water volume of the UVI system, which occupies 1/8 acre of land. If you want a large operation, just increase the number of production units.

Aquaponic systems are not designed with the starting point being the system volume. They are generally designed with the starting point either being the amount of fish you want to produce or the amount of vegetables you want to produce. However, the UVI system volume is apportioned as follows: 8,190 gal (31 m³) for fish production, 17,964 gal (68 m³) for plant production and 2,905 gal (11 m³) for solids removal and other functions.

The answer to your second question can be found in the

following 16-page fact sheet: Recirculating Aquaculture Tank Production Systems: Aquaponics – Integrating Fish and Plant Culture published by the Southern Regional Aquaculture Center (SRAC). The fact sheet gives design problems and shows all the steps required in designing a system from the perspective of the desired fish production or the desired plant production. The key to designing a system is the feeding rate ratio, the weight of feed input to the system in grams per square meter of plant growing area per day. For a raft system this ratio varies from 60 – 100 $g/m^2/day$. It is best to have multiple fish rearing tanks and staggered production cycles so that the amount of feed added to the system on a daily basis is relatively constant. If possible, it is best to stagger plant production too, to even out the uptake of nutrients. Plants such as lettuce and herbs with short production cycles are easier to stagger than large plants such as tomatoes with long production cycles.

In general, the feeding rate ratio of 60 – 100 $g/m^2/day$ works for most plants. The high end of this range would be better for large fruiting plants such as tomatoes or okra. Maintaining the optimum feeding rate ratio is important. In our early work before we knew the correct ratio we added too much feed relative to the plant growing area and experienced a nutrient accumulation problem. Nutrients can accumulate to levels that are toxic to plants. If too little feed is added relative to the plant production area, nutrient deficiencies will occur and result in decreased plant productivity.

➤ Feed rates and plant production

Question

I'm planning to build a commercial system producing culinary herbs (mainly basil). I know that based on what crop you are growing the feeding rate can be anywhere between 28lbs to 47lbs (12.7 – 21.3 kg) of feed/day using the 60-100g/m2 growing area.

1) How do you decide where in this range to go for a crop (staggered production) and still be optimum for the fish? I read in one of your papers that 47lbs (21.3 kg) feed is good for basil production, why is it so high? I don't want to over feed, as feed where I live in Trinidad is expensive.

2) How exactly do you divide 47lbs (21.3 kg) (or whatever the amount you are feeding) of feed between the 4 tanks of fish at different stages of growth and transitions of changing growth?

Answer

Basil is a fast growing crop with a large canopy and requires high levels of nutrients. We did some experiments with basil in batch culture and staggered production. In batch culture all of the plants in the system are transplanted at the same time and are in the same stage of growth. They are all harvested at the same time too. In the last week of a 4-week growth cycle, the plants are growing very rapidly and removing nutrients from the system faster than fish feed via fish digestion can replenish them. We found nutrient deficiencies in batch-cultured basil when the average feeding rate ratio was 69 g/m2 of plant growing area per day.

With staggered production of basil in our system, the plants are in four stages of growth, and at any given time only 25% of the plants are in their final week of growth when the uptake of nutrients is at its highest level. By staggering the production of basil the uptake of nutrients is moderated and nutrient deficiencies

Batch culture of Basil in the UVI raft system

are less likely to occur. The staggered production experiment occurred during the summer when water temperatures were higher and tilapia fed more vigorously. The feeding rate ratio in the staggered production experiment averaged 80 g/m^2/day. Therefore, in the feeding rate ratio range of 60 to 100 g/m^2/day it would be better to be near the upper end of the range for basil. If nutrient levels become too high, a small amount of water exchange (dilution) can lower them.

If you are using the UVI system design and are stocking the fish appropriately (77 Nile tilapia/m^3 to produce 1.8 lb [800 g] fish or 154 red tilapia/m^3 to produce 1.1 lb [500 g fish]), you do not have to overfeed them to obtain a feeding rate ratio near 100 g/m^2/day. Just make sure that you are never underfeeding them. Feed three times a day an amount of feed that they can consume in 30 minutes. Never let them finish the feed faster than 30 minutes, which means they are still hungry and can eat more feed. If that happens, increase the feed allotment, usually in increments of 100 g. Another way to boost the feed consumption is to spread out the feeding times. Instead of feeding them at 9:00 a.m., 1:00 p.m. and 5:00 p.m., you could feed them at 8:00 a.m., 1:00 p.m. and 6:00 p.m. With a longer interval between feedings, they will eat more. When you raise basil, you should feed near the upper end of the range for feeding rate ratios, but you do not have to be exact. Most aquaponically cultured plants do well under a wide range of nutrients levels.

In answer to your second question, you stagger the tilapia production so that the fish are in four stages of growth, and one tank is harvested and restocked every 6 weeks. Each tank should be fed three times a day as described above. The amount of feed to individual tanks will vary considerably over a 24-week growth cycle, but the variation in feeding to the entire system will be less during the 6-week intervals between harvests. There are a lot of approximations in aquaponics, but following these procedures will keep you in the ballpark for good basil and tilapia production.

➢ Ratios for leafy vs. fruiting crops; various fish foods

Question

I've read of the fish-to-plant-ratio formula (57 g feed/m^2 of plant growing area) that you've developed. I have a few questions about this. Is this formula for lettuce, fruiting crops or both? How does the type of fish food factor into this. For instance, would the formula be different for tilapia food than for catfish or trout food? Is it assumed that some of the fish food goes uneaten and breaks down differently than the food that is fully digested and excreted by the fish?

Answer

These are very good and relevant questions. The ratio of 57 g of feed/day/m² of growing area was determined for the staggered production of Bibb lettuce. The Bibb lettuce grew at a rate of 6.2 g/day and some nutrients accumulated in the system over 18 cropping cycles. In our commercial-scale system we staggered the production for loose leaf and romaine lettuce which grew in the range of 0.02 - 0.06 oz (8.9-23.2 g)/day over 28 cropping cycles without significant nutrient accumulation. We are currently producing basil by batch culture (i.e., the entire crop is planted at the same time) at a feeding rate of approximately 100 g/day/m² and we have encountered nutrient deficiencies. Therefore, a higher feeding rate is needed. The optimum feeding rate definitely varies according to the type of crop and the mode of production (i.e., staggered vs. batch culture). Other factors include rate of water exchange, system volume, source-water nutrient levels and the degree and speed of solids removal, which influences mineralization (the release of inorganic nutrients from organic matter during the process of decomposition).

The type of feed will affect the concentration of nutrients to some extent. For example, trout feed has more protein than tilapia or catfish feed and will, therefore, produce higher nitrogen levels in the system, although nitrogen usually occurs in excess with any feed and should be removed through the process of denitrification (i.e., nitrate ions are reduced to nitrogen gas by anaerobic bacteria). Feed manufacturers add varying levels of salt (sodium chloride) to fish feed which affects the concentration of sodium and chloride ions in an aquaponic system. Damon Seawright studied the effect of feed composition on nutrient concentrations in an aquaponic system for his Ph.D. dissertation at the University of Washington. He then developed and tested a "designer diet" that had the right balance of nutrients for hydroponic plant production. Luckily for aquaponic enthusiasts, plants do well within a wide range of nutrient concentrations and ratios between the required nutrients.

In answer to the last part of your question, first of all there should not be a significant amount of uneaten feed. You need to feed at a rate that eliminates or minimizes any wastage of feed. Assuming that some feed goes uneaten, the bacterial-mediated decomposition will be similar to that of the feces, although not exactly the same. The biochemical pathways would be somewhat different for the decomposition of feed because of its higher protein, fat and carbohydrate content. The end result will be the same – the release of inorganic nutrients.

➢ Balance between fish biomass and vegetable production

Question

I have two questions.

1. Are there design parameters that one can use to size the aquaponics component given a fixed fish biomass in a fixed number of tanks? For instance I am thinking of having a shed with six 2,641 gal (10 m³) tanks each containing 33 lb (15kg) of fish per m³. The shed will therefore have 1,984 lb (900 kg) of fish in 15,850 gal (60 m³) of water. What I ask myself is how big should the aquaponics component be for different possible produce that one may consider growing?

2. How does one know that the system is in balance once it is operational? I seem to recall that Dr. Nichols said that the water conductivity is the best measure to determine whether the system is in balance. Would this mean that the conductivity should be same throughout the system, that is, the conductivity of the effluent from the fish tanks should be the same as that of the water at the end of the aquaponics operation? I suspect we will not be in full production for at least five years but hope to receive our first 10,000 fingerlings sooner.

Answer

A density 33 lbs/264 gal (15 kg/m$^{3)}$ is low, but you may be raising a species that cannot tolerate crowding. However, the biomass should not be fixed because presumably the fish will be growing from fingerling to marketable size. My approach to calculating the plant growing area is to estimate the annual and daily feed input to the system. I have to make some assumptions. Let me assume that the growout period for your fish is 24 weeks and the feed conversion ratio (FCR) is 1.7. [FCR is the weight of feed required to produce 1 lb of fish]. Fish production should be staggered so that one tank is harvested every 4 weeks. There will be 13 harvests of 331 lb (150 kg) each (15 kg/m^3 x 10 m^3 per tank). Annual production, annual feed input and daily feed input will be 1,950 kg (150 kg x 13), 3,315 kg (1,950 kg x 1.7) and 9.1 kg (3,315 kg ÷ 365 days). With a daily feed input of 9.1 kg or 9,100 g, the plant growing area for raft culture should be 152 m^2 (9,100 g ÷ 60 g/m^2/day) if a feeding rate ratio of 60 g/m^2/day is selected. The feeding rate ratio is the amount of daily feed input to the system per square meter of plant growing area per day. The optimum feeding rate ratio varies from 60 to 100 g/m^2/day. These ratios cover most produce.

If in some way you are able to maintain a steady biomass of 1,984 lb (900 kg) of fish, then you should determine what your average daily feeding rate is and divide this number in grams by 60 to100g/m^2/day to give the size of the plant growing area. Use the smaller value for small, slow growing plants and the higher value for larger, fast growing plants.

In an aquaponic system that uses rafts for plant production, there will not be any detectable differences in electrical conductivity (an indirect measure of total plant nutrients in the water) at different points in the system. The plants do not remove nutrients fast enough to be detected, and there is a large reservoir of nutrients in the water under the rafts.

➢ Fish to plant ratio for commercial system

Question

I am a student at Ohio State. I am doing a project on aquaponics and I am looking for information on commercial systems. Could you tell me a good ratio for growing beds and fish tanks (how many gal of fish per foot of growing beds)? Also, is aquaponics commercially viable?

Answer

I will answer your question by using the UVI aquaponic system as a reference. A raft-hydroponic, commercial-scale unit has been in continuous operation at the university for more than 10 years. The correct ratio of fish and plant components is determined by the feeding rate ratio, i.e., the daily fish feeding rate per unit of plant growing surface area. In the UVI system we determined that the optimum feeding rate ratio ranges from 60 to 100 g of fish feed per square meter of plant growing area per day. At this ratio most nutrients are maintained at concentrations that maximize plant growth. The system does require supplementation with calcium, potassium and iron.

In designing the system, the fish rearing volume was divided among four tanks so that tilapia production could be staggered, and one tank could be harvested every 6 weeks (the grow-out period for tilapia is 24 weeks).

With this system the amount of feed going into an individual tank will vary considerably over the 24 week period (from a low rate after stocking to a high rate near harvest time), but the amount of feed going into the entire system will fluctuate much less so that the feeding rate ratio is relatively constant.

In the UVI system the ratio of hydroponic tank surface area to fish tank surface area is 7.3:1. The fish and hydroponic tanks have water depths of 3.5 ft (1.07 m) and 1 ft (0.3 m), respectively. The fish tanks are stocked so that the final density at harvest is approximately 0.5 lb/gal.

These are general principles. Designing a system is much more complicated. Recently I revised a fact sheet on aquaponics for the Southern Regional Aquaculture Center. It is SRAC Publication No. 454, Recirculating Aquaculture Tank Production Systems: Aquaponics – Integrating Fish and Plant Culture. This revised fact sheet includes some sample problems that will help you design a commercial system.

Aquaponics is commercially viable provided there is a good market for the type of fish and plants being raised and the system is designed correctly and operated efficiently. Considerable knowledge and planning is needed before a commercial operation is launched.

➢ Fish to plant ratio with seedlings

Question

I have a query about the feed to plant ratio. The ratio you have established for plants in a raft system (60-100 g/m²) is based on the plants entering the system as established seedlings.

If these seedlings were to be grown from seed in the system more space would need to be allowed to factor this slow growth rate time from germination to seedling size.

For example if seeds take 3 weeks from sowing to reach seedling size, and then 6 weeks to maturity, in a system where seeds are started in situ, would not approximately 50% more plant area need to be set aside to factor in this initial slow growth rate? Also, what do you think is the best ratio to use in a gravel filled system?

Answer

I think it is better to start the seedlings in a separate system of trays and a growing media such as a mixture of coir (coconut fiber) and vermiculite. If you start the seedlings in the system, the environment may be too wet initially for the delicate sprouting seeds. Too much water and low oxygen promote the growth of fungus, which can kill seedlings. This is called damping off disease. In our greenhouse, we water the sprouting seeds only once a day so that moisture is not excessive and there is plenty of air (containing oxygen) in the growing medium.

Let's say you could start seedlings in the system. Your question implies that nutrients would be too high initially if the feeding rate ratio was 60-100 g/m^2/day. I think what you are saying is that by holding feed input to the system constant and increasing the plant growing area, the feeding rate ratio would decline and be more in balance with the nutrient uptake by the small seedlings. That's true if the feed input is held constant. Another way of decreasing the ratio is by reducing feed input to the system while the seedlings are becoming established and nutrient requirements are low.

➢ Ratios in gravel and NFT (nutrient film technique)

Question

I have recently read the Southern Regional Aquaculture Center report entitled, "Recirculating Aquaculture Tank Production Systems: Aquaponics-Integrating Fish and Plant Culture", which you authored along with Michael P Masser and Thomas M Lasordo. This is an excellent publication.

I have a question about comments you made about NFT aquaponic systems. It was stated that, "Gravel and NFT systems should have a feeding ratio that is approximately 25 percent of the recommended ratio for raft aquaponics." Does this conversely mean that with a given volume of fish tanks and fish biomass, you can have four times more space in plant production in an NFT system than in a raft system?

Answer

The answer to your question is yes. In the fact sheet I explained that in raft culture (deep flowing technique) about 75% of the system's water is in the hydroponic tanks. Let's say as an example that the system has 4,000 gal (15.1 m^3) of water. Then 3,000 gal (11.36 m^3) would be in the hydroponic tanks and 1,000 gal (3.8 m^3) would be in the rest of the system. Let's further say that a feeding rate ratio of 100 g of fish feed per 1 m^2 of plant growing area per day maintains optimum nutrient levels for plant growth. In nutrient film technique (NFT) and gravel systems there is very little water in the hydroponic component. Therefore, an NFT or gravel system producing a similar amount of fish would have slightly more than 1,000 gal of water.

In this example I will assume that additional biofiltration will be added to maintain water quality. If a feeding rate ratio of 100 g/m2/day is used in this system, it is logical to assume that nutrients would accumulate to a level that is approximately four times higher than that in the raft system, which is the optimum level, and the higher concentration in the NFT and gravel systems would most likely be toxic to plants.

Therefore, to maintain optimum nutrient levels, the feeding rate ratio should be reduced to 25 g/m^2/day, which would cause a 75% reduction in fish production, or the plant growing area should be four times larger, which would not decrease fish production but would increase plant production substantially.

➢ Barramundi to basil ratio

Question

I want to design a large commercial-scale aquaponics facility. We need to produce 50 ton/year barramundi (Lates calcarifer) at 17.6 oz (500 g) harvest size. If, for example, at any time the farm holds 30 ton barramundi, what is the best way of determining the quantity of plants we can produce (we'll be growing basil in NFT channels), in terms of nutrient levels? Is there a ballpark formula that can be used? Otherwise, what considerations should we make in figuring this out? Any help would be greatly appreciated.

Answer

I will try to give you an approximate answer. Let's assume the feed conversion ratio for barramundi is 1.5. In other words, 1.5 lb of food is required to produce 1 lb of growth. Discounting the initial weight of fingerlings, the amount of food required to produce 50 metric tons (mt) of barramundi would be 75 mt per year or 0.205 mt per day, which equals 452 lb (205,000 g). In raft hydroponics, we know that the approximate daily feeding rate ratio for good basil production is 100 g/m^2 of plant growing area. I will assume that the same plant density is used for the NFT system. However, the NFT system has very little water in the troughs while a raft aquaponic system has approximately 75% of its water in the hydroponic tanks, which are 0.98 ft (30 cm) deep. Therefore, the total water volume of the NFT system is only about 25% of the water volume of the raft system. If the same feeding rate ratio was used, nutrient concentrations would be four times higher and could reach toxic levels. I therefore assume that the correct feeding rate ratio for an NFT basil system would be about 25 g/m^2/day.

Note that there are many assumptions here which should be verified through production trials. If the average daily feeding rate is 205,000 g, then the required plant growing area would be 8,200 m^2 (205,000 g divided by 25 g/m^2 = 8,200 m^2).

In the UVI system, basil is planted at a density of 16 plants/m2 and cultured for 8 weeks in the system. It is harvested after four weeks by cutting the main stems and allowed to re-grow for another 4 weeks before it is entirely harvested. A growing area of 88,264 ft^2 (8,200 m^2) would require 131,200 plants every 8 weeks under ideal conditions. Of course this production figure would require environmental control in temperate regions. During winter the culture period would be longer due to lower light intensity and fewer plants would be needed. It would be best to stagger the production of basil so that a portion of the production area is harvested weekly.

➤ Fish ratio and biomass

Question

I have been studying the chapter on aquaponics that you wrote in the book "Recirculating Aquaculture Systems." On page 641, there is a chart that shows a feed ratio of 1.4 for Nile tilapia. At 2 oz (57 g) per day per m^2 of raft tank area, that would be an input of 6.72 lb (3.05 kg) per tank or 26.9 lb (12.2 kg) for all four tanks, per day. That input per day in each tank doesn't come out to a feed ratio of 1.4 as the chart shows. What am I doing wrong in my calculations?

If the feed ratio is 1.4 and the final biomass is 168 lb (76 kg)/ m^3 and you subtract the initial weight of the stocked fish, you get a daily input of 3 oz (84 g)/ per square meter of raft area. On page 656 it states that at 84 grams of feed input per day, your production dropped in Bibb lettuce production.

Answer

I think this data represents different experiments and systems. The system does not need exact feeding rates. And the number of

57 g/m^2/day came from one experiment more than 15 years ago. Now I say 60-100 g/m^2/day. This is just ballpark. What I do for the commercial system is select the annual production capacity. Our experience shows that 11,000 lbs (4,990 kg) is possible. The FCR (feed conversion ratio) for Nile tilapia is now 1.7. (The 1.4 came from a trial when we were paying much closer attention to feeding. It might have been a higher protein feed. I remember once we used 40%+ protein instead of our normal 32%).

So, I take 11,000 x 1.7 = 18,700 lbs of feed per year divided by 365 days = 51.2 lbs per day x 454 g per lb = 23,245 g divided by our 214 m2 of surface area = 108.6 g per m^2 per day. That's slightly out of range. However, we now discharge all the water from the filter tanks when we clean so water exchange is higher than it was before. Our TDS level was 236 ppm (mg/liter) during our recent okra trial. It's usually below 500 ppm (mg/liter). That 3.8 oz (108.6 g) per m^2 per day is just an average. It will be higher just before harvest and lower after harvest.

The beauty of having deep channels is the large reservoir of nutrients. You do not need fine control. This will make life difficult. Measure TDS or EC. If TDS is too low, then don't exchange so much water. If we dump our filter tanks twice a week, that's a loss of 800 gal (3 m^3) or 2.7% of system volume. I am considering draining this water slowly and returning it to the system to raise TDS. You want TDS in a range of 200-2,000, although I prefer to work at the lower end (<1,000 TDS) of this range. The system has great latitude. It does not have to be as exact as hydroponics. All you need to measure is pH and TDS (EC).

Fish Health

➢ Slow growing fish

Question

I have an aquaponics system that I have been struggling with and was wondering if you might have some insight. It is a media bed style, in a poly tunnel. There is one 300 gal (1.1 m³) tank where the fish grow to harvest, one smaller tank for fry, one smaller tank for females to have their babies. There are 3 – 4 ft x 8 ft (2.4 m x 1.2 m) media beds and we've grown peppers, herbs and lettuce so far. We got one good harvest of fish the first year we started. Now the fish (tilapia) do not seem to be growing hardly at all. I suspected old feed to start with but with new feed they do not seem to be doing any better.

On top of this heating costs (especially in the winter) are quite high and I am wondering if I could do better with a colder water fish than tilapia. I was wondering about carp – would they be a better choice?

Answer

Water quality will affect fish growth. Low water temperature will slow tilapia growth appreciably if the temperature is in the 70-80°F (21-26.6°C) range. Tilapia prefer water temperature around 85°F (29.4°C). Parasites or disease will make tilapia go "off feed" where they stop feeding entirely. Usually this situation leads to some mortality. Very high nitrate levels (>700 ppm (mg/liter)) as nitrate-nitrogen) will slow feed consumption and growth. Some unknown toxic compound in your water supply could be affecting your fish but not killing them. This compound could be affecting the nitrifying bacteria, which would result in elevated levels of ammonia and nitrite that are not high enough to kill the fish but high enough to affect their growth. Concentrations of total ammonia-nitrogen and nitrite-nitrogen should be 1 mg/liter or less. Low dissolved oxygen (DO) levels will affect fish growth. Maintain DO at 5 ppm (mg/liter) or higher for maximum growth. Feed could be an issue if it is stored for several months, especially at high temperatures. Essential nutrients in the feed such as vitamin C break down over time and fish feed oils become rancid.

Another problem with feed is the possible presence molds in the feed or in the feed ingredients. Some species of commonly occurring fungi produce a toxin known as aflatoxin, which causes a disease in fish called aflatoxicosis. The ingredients of feed such as peanut meal, corn, wheat, sunflower, or soybeans can be contaminated with aflatoxins. Feed manufacturers screen for aflatoxins, but screening all grains is difficult as the international trade in feed grains increases, especially in the tropics where warm, moist conditions favor the growth of fungi. In tilapia and catfish feeds there is also a trend to use more plant-based ingredients which increases the potential of aflatoxicosis. Studies with Nile tilapia showed that low concentrations of aflatoxin B1 decreased growth without noticeable signs of mortality.

Signs of aflatoxicosis include pale gills, impaired blood clotting, anemia, poor growth rates or lack of weight gain. Prolonged exposure can cause liver tumors and mortality. Aflatoxins can also destroy essential nutrients such as vitamin A, C and thiamin, which can lead to nutrient deficiency diseases, loss of immunity and reduced growth.

It is important to buy fresh feed and use it up within 3 months. Feed should be stored under cool or refrigerated conditions with humidity control to create a dry environment. Feed bags should be placed on pallets in a clean area at least 1 ft (0.3 m) from the wall to avoid condensation. If feed contains a blue/grey mold, clumps together and smells musty, it should be discarded.

Even if you switch to a cool water fish these factors could

affect them too and should be considered.

Trout is a good candidate for a fish that can grow at lower water temperatures. The optimum temperature range for rainbow trout is 55-65°F (12.7–18.3°C). Maintain water temperature at the upper end of this range (65°F/18.3°C) for good vegetable growth. There is a substantial ornamental fish market for koi carp, which grows suitably at lower water temperatures. Most species of carp are not accepted as food fish in the U.S. However, grass carp has white firm flesh and is considered a delicacy. It grows rapidly and can reach sizes of 30 lbs (13.6 kg) or more on a diet of aquatic plants. They will even eat terrestrial plants. They also grow rapidly on formulated diets (pellets). In the U.S. you would need to buy grass carp that are certified as being sterile, and you should check with officials to see if they are legal in your state. Grass carp like to jump so your rearing tank should be covered with a net. Grass carp have Y-shaped intramuscular bones like northern pike, but these bones present no problem when the fish is large.

➢ Managing fish disease in tilapia

Question

We have just started a small aquaponic system with tilapia and I was just wondering about your experiences with mortality rates for the fry and how you manage diseases. A few of the fry we got came with what I think is pop eye (clouding of one or both eyes) and bacterial fin disease. We have separated them in a hospital tank and started treatment with triple sulfa antibiotic from a pet store. Does this work? Should I give any preventive treatment for the healthy looking fish that were exposed to the sick ones? Should I completely change the water and clean out the system?

Answer

The sick fish probably have a bacterial disease. Some common diseases that can affect tilapia are motile Aeromonas septicmia (*Aeromonas hydrophila* and related species), Pseudomonas septicemia (*Pseudomonas fluorescence*), vibriosis (*Vibrio anguillarum* and related species), columnaris (*Flavobacterium columnare*), edwardsiellosis (*Edwardsiella tarda*) and streptococcosis (*Streptococcus* spp.). Because the clinical signs of most of these diseases are similar, it is necessary to isolate the causative bacterium and culture it on laboratory media for exact identification. Several of these bacteria are usually present in freshwater and they generally cause a secondary infection in response to a stress such as rough handling, a decrease in water temperature or high organic loads.

Once the infection sets in, it usually proceeds until the fish dies. However, if the stress is removed, the fish may recover. Your fish were probably stressed during shipment. If you order fish again you should purchase them from another supplier. The sick fish can be cured with antibiotics such as Terramycin®, Romet-30® or Erythromycin®. Romet-30® contains sulfur and may be similar to the drug you purchased. These antibiotics are incorporated into feed at a concentration of 50 mg/kg and fed for 5 days with Romet-30® or 12 days with the other two antibiotics. However, there are no therapeutic agents approved by FDA for tilapia at the present time. You would need an "extra-label use" permit which, in certain instances, can be provided by a veterinarian.

I suggest you let nature take its course with your sick fish. Isolating them is a good idea. Changing the water will not help as all your fish have already been exposed to water containing the sick fish. To prevent further disease you should maintain a high quality environment and practice good fish health management. Maintain a reasonable density (no more than 0.5 lbs/gal). Provide adequate dissolved oxygen levels (>5 mg/L).

Keep total ammonia-nitrogen and nitrite-nitrogen below 1 ppm (mg/liter). Maintain water temperature around 85°F (29.4°C). Do not overfeed or let organic matter accumulate in the rearing tank. Do not use the same net for both sick and healthy fish. Disinfect the net and other utensils by dipping them into 200 ppm (mg/liter) of chlorine or in 100 ppm (mg/liter) of a quaternary ammonium compound (RoccalTM, HyaminTM, benzalkonium chloride, etc.). Iodine at 1000 ppm (mg/liter) is another disinfectant that may be safer to use than chlorine or ammonium. Drying nets and utensils will also kill most pathogens. A trait that makes tilapia so attractive for culture is its hardiness and resistance to parasites and diseases. It is unusual for tilapia to get sick under good growing conditions.

Plant Health

➤ Determining nutrient deficiencies or toxicities

Question

Can plants be used to determine the chemical aspects of the water in an aquaponic system? For instance, we know that low nitrogen will show certain results in lettuce (not very green and not much growth). So, what happens when there is too much or too little of the other key elements? Can observation of plant health be used to determine nutrient problems? The reason I'm asking is that I do not wish to use any test equipment to determine the quality of the water because I need to keep the system as low cost as possible.

Answer

Plants will tell you through various abnormalities when they are suffering from a nutrient deficiency or toxicity. However, the message they give is not always clear. Several of the symptoms look similar and, if two nutrients are deficient or toxic, the symptoms are very unclear. Dr. Howard Resh, in his book, "Hydroponic Food Production: a Definitive Guidebook for the Advanced Home Gardener and the Commercial Hydroponic Grower", writes as follows: "When two or more elements are deficient simultaneously, the composite picture or syndrome expressed by the symptoms may resemble no given deficiency. Under such conditions it is generally impossible to determine visually which elements are responsible for the symptoms." Dr. Resh does offer a key to identify mineral deficiency symptoms and lists the deficiency and toxicity symptoms of the essential elements. He describes in detail the mineral deficiency symptoms of tomatoes and cucumbers. The book, "Nutritional Disorders in Glasshouse Tomatoes, Cucumbers and Lettuce" by J.P.N.L. Roorda van Eysunga and K.W. Smilde, is very useful because it provides pictures of nutrient deficiency and toxicity symptoms of tomatoes, cucumbers and lettuce.

In general, the approach you suggest is not sound due to the difficulty of identifying the element or elements causing the deficiency or toxicity. Fortunately, if aquaponic systems are designed correctly, operated with the optimum ratio of daily feed input to plant growing area and supplemented with calcium, potassium and iron as prescribed, there should not be any nutrient deficiencies or toxicities. I can only speak for the UVI system, with which I have the greatest experience. We never have a toxicity problem. In doing research, very rarely does a deficiency problem occur. We have solved any isolated deficiency problem by adding more fish feed though intensive feed management or by switching to a staggered plant production system to moderate nutrient demand. (In the opposing production system – batch culture – all plants reach maturity at the same time and exert a high rate of nutrient uptake that could deplete the supply of some nutrients in spite of the fact that nutrients are generated daily in aquaponics.) During a 3-year trial with leaf lettuce production, no nutrient deficiencies were observed. Although we analyzed water quality variables for research purposes, these analyses would not have been necessary for a commercial producer.

In the unlikely event that you encounter a deficiency or toxicity problem in your system, a water sample and a leaf tissue sample could be sent to a commercial laboratory for analysis at a reasonable cost. After the causative element or elements are identified, you could modify your operating procedure and avoid the need for subsequent analyses.

➢ Compost Tea

Question

I am an organic gardener and would like to set up a small aquaponic system. In organic gardening, I make compost tea that I spray on the plant leaves and soil. This provides necessary bacteria to the soil and nutrients to the plants. Is this a practice I should use in my aquaponic set up?

Answer

That process is not necessary in an aquaponic system. The water in the aquaponic system is in essence a compost tea. The water becomes brown in color due to the decomposition of organic matter, primarily fish feces, which contain large quantities of indigestible plant material. The major components of fish feed are soybeans and corn. The dark color represents humic substances, such as tannic acid, that are not easily broken down by microorganisms. These substances have mild antibiotic properties that protect both the fish and the plants from pathogens.

The culture water has the right balance of most of the nutrients required for good plant growth with the exception of calcium, potassium and iron. It is best to supplement calcium and potassium as calcium hydroxide and potassium hydroxide in the process of pH control. Iron could be supplemented as a foliar spray. However, it is probably easier to add chelated iron to the water at a concentration of 2 ppm (mg/liter) once every 3 weeks. The roots of plants grown in an aquaponic system absorb the nutrients that you supplement as a foliar spray using a compost tea.

➢ Potassium deficiency

Question

We have a 1,000 gal (3.8 m³) tank for the fish (tilapia) and 6 beds about 5 ft X 9 ft (1.5 m x 2.7 m). We are currently growing tomatoes, cucumbers and various herbs, mostly basil. I believe I have a potassium deficiency in our tomato plants and would like to know how to maintain the balance needed in our aquaponic system to grow tomatoes. Any information that you could give us would be greatly appreciated.

Answer

It would be helpful if I knew the type of aquaponic system, aggregate (e.g., gravel) or raft. I'm going to guess that it is pea gravel and that you do not remove solids. Since the solids stay in the system and decompose, you obtain sufficient inorganic nutrients through the process of mineralization, the microbial breakdown and release of inorganic chemicals from organic matter. The gravel acts as a biofilter and the nitrifying bacteria in the gravel remove ammonia and nitrite and produce nitrate. This process is called nitrification and it produces acid. Calcium carbonate is probably a component of the gravel. The calcium carbonate dissolves to neutralize the acid and buffer your system.

In the UVI raft system, which does not contain gravel, we must supplement calcium, potassium and iron. These nutrients are not obtained in sufficient quantities from fish feed. In your situation you obtain adequate calcium from the dissolution of calcium carbonate. Your source water may have sufficient iron. (Often water has too much iron if it is pumped from a well.) But you do not have any source of potassium unless you supplement this nutrient. We maintain our pH at 7.0-7.5 through the alternate addition of calcium hydroxide and potassium hydroxide, thereby supplementing both calcium and potassium, but you do not have a need for adding base because base is part of the gravel. Therefore, you must supplement potassium in some other form.

The two best forms of potassium for your system are potassium nitrate (KNO_3) or potassium sulfate (K_2SO_4). Tomatoes need high levels of potassium. I suggest that you aim for a potassium concentration of approximately 100 ppm (mg/liter). However, you already have sufficient nitrate and sulfate concentrations from the fish effluent so you do not want to add too much of these compounds.

Your 1,000-gal fish tank contains 3,785 liters of water. Let me round up to 4,000 liters. The atomic weight of potassium is 38.7% of the molecular weight of KNO_3 and 44.9 % of the molecular weight of K_2SO_4. To determine the quantity of these compounds that must be added to obtain a potassium concentration of 100 mg/liter, use the following equations:

($KNO_3 = x$)
(0.387)(x) = 100 mg/liter
x = 100 mg/liter divided by 0.387
x = 258 mg/liter
(258 mg/liter)(4000 liters) = 1,032,000 mg
1,032,000 mg divided by 1000 mg/g = 1032 g

($K_2SO_4 = x$)
(0.449)(x) = 100 mg/liter
x = 100 mg/liter divided by 0.449
x = 223 mg/liter
(223 mg/liter)(4000 liters) = 892,000 mg
892,000 mg divided by 1000 mg/g = 892 g

If you add 2.27 lbs (1032 g) of KNO_3, you will increase the nitrate-nitrogen concentration by 38.8 ppm (mg/liter) (the term nitrate-nitrogen expresses just the weight of nitrogen in the nitrate ion). If you add 1.96 lbs (892 g) of K_2SO_4, you will increase the sulfate (SO_4) concentration by 122.8 ppm (mg/liter). I suggest adding half the amount required for each of these compounds. You do not want to add too much nitrogen because this will lead to excessive vegetative growth and low fruit set. After adding these compounds, do not add again until potassium deficiencies reappear.

Muriate of potash (KCl) is another compound that could be used to correct potassium deficiencies. It has a high percentage (52.4%) of potassium, but it should only be used if there are low levels of sodium chloride (less than 50 ppm (mg/liter)) in the water. Adding chloride in the presence of sodium is toxic to plants, although tomatoes have a much higher tolerance to sodium chloride than other hydroponic plants.

➤ Lanky Lettuce

Question

I am an agriculture teacher looking for help. My class and I have set up 2 recirculating aquaculture systems in which we currently are raising koi and tilapia. We have experimented with running the water through an NFT type system but the lettuce we grew appears long and lanky. We are in a greenhouse with extra plant lights. Could it be the heat?

Also, the nitrate levels are between 20 and 50 ppm (mg/liter) and the ammonia nitrogen levels remain low, between 1 and 2 ppm (mg/liter) because of the biofilter and bubble bead filter. I am new so, whatever you can tell me would be great.

Answer

You do not have a nutrition problem and you do not have a heat problem unless your plants are bolting, sending up seed stalks.

Lettuce plants that grow long and lanky usually do not have sufficient light. At UVI we once used 30% shade cloth over our lettuce as a barrier to insects. Even though we have intense solar radiation in the Virgin Islands, the plants elongated and grew in a spiral fashion. You may need more light.

Another factor is the planting density. The plants may be too close together so that there is competition for light, which causes the plants to grow tall and spindly. Bibb lettuce should be planted on 7 inch (17.8 cm) centers. There should be 7 inches of space between a plant and its neighboring plants in every direction. Leaf lettuce requires more space. We plant leaf lettuce 8 inches (20.3 cm) apart in rows that are 12 inches (30.5 cm) apart. Romaine lettuce requires even more space.

First, see if the spacing is your problem before adding more lights, because adding lights is a much more costly solution.

Environmental Considerations

➤ Growing on the coastline of Mexico

Question

I wish to establish a medium-size system in Oaxaca on some land I have. It is hot here most of the time between 77-104°F (25-40°C). Basically, in doing research I have come across a couple of questions I hope you can help me with.

Firstly, would a greenhouse be necessary in the tropics or would I really need a similar structure but with shading material rather than normal greenhouse material?

Secondly, I live right on the coast and have access to sea water with salts that contain valuable minerals. Can I assume that a small ratio say, 20-to-1 saltwater/freshwater would aid in supplying trace minerals to the fish and then the plants without any detrimental effect on those organisms?

Thirdly, do the fish tanks need to be in the shade?

Answer

High temperatures of 104°F (40°C) or greater would present a challenge, especially for crops such as lettuce, but you could use crops that do well at high temperatures. Finding the crops that do best under your temperature regime may require some experimentation. You may also have to consider using some sort of seasonal crop rotation or just a fallow period (no crops) during the hottest months of the year.

In the UVI system we initially painted our polystyrene sheets a light blue until I put a thermometer on a sheet one afternoon. The surface temperature was about 104°F (40°C). Light blue really absorbs heat. We then repainted the sheets white, which lowered the surface temperature about 10°F. When the sheets were blue, lettuce plants still grew, but they wilted during the hottest part of the day. This obviously slowed their growth. We find that sweet basil, watermelon, cantaloupe and okra do well at high temperatures. There are probably many other plants do will do well too. Water temperature is more important than air temperature. If you have cool nights, which lowers the water temperature, the plants will respond better to daytime heat.

Building a greenhouse will add considerable capital and operating costs. You would have to add evaporative cooling pads or fogging systems to maintain suitable greenhouse temperatures. There are also greenhouses with computer control systems that automatically open the sides on cool days for natural ventilation. These are standard technologies, but they will increase the management complexity. Pursue this technology if you have the capital and a market for your product that will earn a profit.

The main constituent of saltwater is sodium chloride and this compound is detrimental to plants. Some plants, like tomatoes, can tolerate higher salinity but I would not suggest using diluted saltwater.

You should definitely shade your fish tanks. No part of an aquaponic system should have exposure to direct sunlight because the light will stimulate the growth of algae. Aquaponic systems are engineered to direct nutrients to valuable terrestrial plants (vegetables, culinary herbs, flowers) instead of algae, which can cause problems by coating plant roots or clogging screens. Fish prefer subdued light, especially in the clear water of aquaponic systems. Covering the fish also helps to lower water temperature.

➤ Aquaponics in Dubai and other desert countries

Question

Please advise me if working in aquaponic culture is preferred in a country like Dubai.

Answer

I imagine Dubai has amazingly hot summers and cool winters. These conditions would require an environment-controlled greenhouse with some heating in the winter and lots of cooling at the peak of the summer. If hydroponic greenhouse production occurs in Dubai, and I assume it does, then aquaponics will work just fine. One of our former short course students built a UVI (University of the Virgin Islands) aquaponic system in Riyadh, Saudi Arabia at the King Abdulaziz City of Science and Technology. According to the latest information I received, it was working well, producing tilapia and lettuce. A recent graduate of our short course (June, 2002) is currently building a UVI aquaponic system near Antelias, Lebanon. What is exciting about his system is that he is building all of the tanks with concrete as opposed to fiberglass which is often used in aquaponic systems but is much more expensive.

In a country like Dubai, aquaponics is an ideal way to raise fish and plants because water is conserved and reused, nutrients are recycled and discharged sludge can be used to irrigate and fertilize field crops. Water-use efficiency with aquaponics is exceedingly high, more so than standard recirculating aquaculture systems or standard hydroponics. In a country with scarce freshwater resources, this is a great advantage in reducing production costs. In addition, the low water requirements of aquaponic systems permit the cost-effective use of desalinated water. During droughts we purchase desalinated water for our systems. Normally we obtain water from rainwater catchments. Although environmental control is expensive, I assume that low electric rates in Dubai, due to abundant oil supplies, would offset some of the operating costs. Evaporative cooling pads can be operated with saltwater, thereby saving precious fresh water.

My final assumption is that fresh, high quality fish and vegetables command very high prices in Dubai. Aquaponic systems could be located in close proximity to markets. Products from these systems would reach markets faster and in better condition than imported products and they would not incur the transportation costs of imported products. Given all these factors, I think that commercial aquaponic operations would be an attractive investment in Dubai.

➤ Heating with methane

Question

I'm wondering if an aquaponics business could be viable by using the methane from feedlots or chicken farms as a source of energy to heat greenhouses.

Answer

The answer is yes. You can use methane gas as an energy source for heating greenhouses. The methane can be produced from the decomposition of animal wastes or from garbage buried in landfills. The New Jersey EcoComplex, which is managed by Rutgers University, uses methane gas from a nearby landfill to operate a boiler that heats a 46,000 ft^2 (4,274 m^2) greenhouse. As part of a recent project between Rutgers University and the University of the Virgin Islands, four microturbines were installed next to the greenhouse to generate 120 kW of electricity, which is used to operate an aquaponic system, high-pressure sodium lamps during the winter and other equipment (see article describing this project in Aquaponics Journal, Vol. 7, No. 1, pages 22-25). The microturbines are fueled by methane gas from the landfill. Methane gas should be processed to remove impurities (carbon dioxide, hydrogen sulfide) and water vapor. If the moisture content of the methane is too high, it can extinguish the flame in a boiler for example. Sensors and phone alarms are required to notify the operator if a boiler stops operating. I imagine it would be quite unpleasant to be woken up and have to leave home at 2:00 a.m. on a subzero night to relight a boiler flame.

> ## Carbon dioxide generation

Question

I enjoyed reading Dr. Rakocy's article "UVI Aquaponics Heads North to New Jersey." It was detailed and, as usual, very informative. The question it evoked is: when designing an aquaponics system for an enclosed greenhouse environment, is there a rule of thumb for the amount of carbon dioxide that a given area of plant bed can absorb versus fish rearing tank surface area? I realize that there are many variables, plant type etc. I'm just looking for a design rule of thumb.

Answer

Plants utilize carbon dioxide (CO_2), absorbed from the atmosphere through openings (stomata) in their leaves, and water, absorbed by their roots, to manufacture glucose through a process called photosynthesis. Glucose supplies energy and plant building material, which is transformed into many chemical compounds to create plant structure and growth. Increasing the concentration of CO_2 in the atmosphere can increase crop yields by approximately 30%. Carbon dioxide enhancement is widely practiced in the enclosed environment of greenhouses. Carbon dioxide generation takes place in a device that burns LP or natural gas. Carbon dioxide can also be injected into the greenhouse from a cylinder of compressed CO_2.

The fish component of an aquaponic system is a CO_2 generator. The feed consumed by the fish is digested and then burned in cells to create energy. The waste products of this chemical reaction are water and CO_2 gas. The gas is transferred into the culture water through the gills. Additional CO_2 is produced through the microbial decomposition of organic matter in the system. Carbon dioxide is vented into the atmosphere by the aeration system. If the amount of gas generated is significant, it could contribute to increased vegetable yields. To my knowledge no one has documented the effect of recycled CO_2 from an aquaponic system on plant growth. I will attempt to quantify CO_2 production and determine if it is significant with respect to CO_2 enhancement.

The concentration of CO_2 in air is 0.035% or 350 ppm (mg/liter). The amount of carbon dioxide required to enhance plant production varies and depends on many factors. At the EcoComplex at Rutgers University, where we installed a UVI aquaponic system, CO_2 generation units are designed to produce a maximum CO_2 concentration of 1,500 ppm (mg/liter) to stimulate the production of tomatoes in a tightly constructed greenhouse with supplemental lighting and no ventilation. Let's substitute aquaponics for the CO_2 generator. A rule of thumb is that each unit of feed by weight will eventually result in the production of one unit of CO2 by weight. Assuming that the annual net production of tilapia is 7,500 lbs (3,401 kg) and the feed conversion ratio is 1.5, 11,250 lbs (5,103 kg) of feed will be added to the system annually. Dividing by 365 days year, the average daily feed ration will be 30.8 lbs (14 kg). Therefore, approximately 30.8 lbs of CO_2 will be generated daily. The greenhouse was 170 ft x 36 ft x 15 ft (51.8 m x 11 m x 4.6 m). The volume of the greenhouse is 91,800 ft^3 (2,600 m^3). At 70°F

(21.1°C) and an elevation of 1,000 ft (305 m), a cubic meter of air weighs 2.6 lbs (1,162 g). The total weight of air in the greenhouse is therefore 1,162 g/m3 x 2,600 m3 or 3,021,000 g, which can be rounded off to 3,000,000 g. The weight in grams of CO_2 generated daily over the weight in grams of air in the greenhouse is 13,983/3,000,000. Dividing both the numerator and the denominator by 3 converts this expression to 4,661/1,000,000 or 4,661 ppm. A very tight greenhouse will exchange 25% of its air volume without outside air per hour. There will be approximately six air volume exchanges per day. Dividing 4,661 ppm by 6 equals 777 ppm of CO_2, which represents the steady state level of CO_2 enhancement. Adding this level of enhancement with the ambient CO_2 concentration (350 ppm) equals 1127 ppm, a level that is 75% of the target CO_2 concentration for enhancement. This calculation could be verified by measuring CO_2 levels in a well-sealed aquaponic greenhouse. The amount of CO_2 generated daily from this aquaponic system should stimulate plant growth. The increased growth and yield may be high enough to eliminate the fuel-burning CO_2 generator, thereby saving both the cost of fuel and the cost of a generator, which would be another major advantage of aquaponics. The advantage of aquaponic CO_2 generation needs to be verified and quantified experimentally.

The rule thumb then concerning aquaponic CO_2 generation is this: If an aquaponic system in a tightly enclosed greenhouse environment is designed for the optimum feeding rate ratio (e.g., 57-100 g/day/m2), the system will provide CO_2 enhancement, which will stimulate plant growth and increase production.

Nutrient Availability for Plants

➢ Nitrification vs. denitrification

Question

Can you explain the difference between denitrifying bacteria and anaerobic ones? When talking about nitrates and bio-digesters, there are 2 paths we can take, anaerobic or aerobic; it is said that aerobic digestion will blow off a lot of your nitrogen and that anaerobic is better in that it will help conserve the nitrogen... well what is the difference then between denitrification and anaerobic bacteria...denitrification will turn your NO_3 into NO_2 and N_2 gas and of course other things...as an end result, you lose nitrogen. How can anaerobic digestion prevent this from happening...or should I say, how can we prevent denitrification in our anaerobic digesters?

Answer

The correct comparisons are nitrifying bacteria vs. denitrifying bacteria and aerobic bacteria (requiring oxygen) vs. anaerobic bacteria (requiring the absence of oxygen). Nitrifying bacteria convert toxic ammonia to toxic nitrite followed by the conversion of nitrite to relatively non-toxic nitrate. Nitrifying bacteria are aerobic bacteria. They require oxygen. Denitrifying bacteria convert nitrate to nitrogen gas when oxygen is absent. Denitrifying bacteria are anaerobic bacteria. The nitrogen gas gradually diffuses into the atmosphere. Therefore, when aquaculture effluent is digested anaerobically, all of the nitrogen in nitrate ions is eventually lost to the atmosphere. A small amount of ammonium and nitrite ions remain as the only source of inorganic nitrogen. Let me give you an example. Before we installed denitrification channels in our biofloc system, nitrate-nitrogen levels reached peak values of close to 700 ppm (mg/liter). These levels of nitrate can affect fish health and growth, and that is why we added a denitrification process. Prior to adding the channels, we tested the efficacy of denitrification. Sludge was placed in an un-aerated tank for 2 days. It quickly became anaerobic and nitrate-nitrogen levels decreased to 0 ppm (mg/liter).

Aerobic digestion is the best method for preventing the loss of inorganic nitrogen. If the aquaculture effluent is aerated vigorously to maintain some dissolved oxygen in the sludge, the conversation of nitrate ions to nitrogen gas by denitrifying bacteria will be slowed but not stopped. Anaerobic conditions may occur within the center of the sludge particles, which will lead to some denitrification.

➢ Nutrient availability and lowering pH

Question

I read that you supplement potassium and calcium when you raise pH but what about other elements, like nitrogen, iron and phosphorous? Also, I have a problem with my pH going up, not down. So what should I add to lower pH without killing the fish? Can I add some kind of acid? And, if that product doesn't have calcium and potassium in it, what do I add to supplement those? I currently have a small system in my backyard and I raise some tilapia and vegetables. There aren't many fish in the tank so sometimes the nutrient levels are low. I want to add these elements, as needed, rather than stock my tank with too many fish

Answer

Generally we supplement potassium, calcium and iron. However, if your source water has high levels of these nutrients, you may not have to supplement all of them. If you operate your system at a lower pH such as 6.0-6.5, you may not have to supplement iron as often because it is less likely to precipitate out of solution. However, in a heavily fed system that generates a large amount of ammonia (a product of protein metabolism excreted by the fish through their gills), a higher pH (7.0) is better for ammonia removal through the process of nitrification, which is mediated by bacteria, produces acid and lowers pH.

pH goes up in hydroponic systems because plant roots excrete alkaline compounds and there is no oxidative nitrification to counteract this process as in aquaponic systems. Another source of alkalinity is the process of denitrification whereby nitrate ions, the final product of nitrification, are reduced to nitrogen gas under anaerobic conditions, producing an alkaline compound in the process. Therefore, either your system is acting as a hydroponic system with the fish playing a very minor role or there are large accumulations of anaerobic sludge where denitrification is occurring. You can lower the pH by adding nitric acid (which adds nitrogen) or sulfuric acid (which adds sulfur) or phosphoric acid (which adds phosphorus) or hydrochloric acid (but too much chloride is detrimental to plant growth). Substantially dilute the concentrated acid solution sold by suppliers before adding it to the aquaponic system. Take a water sample and determine the amount of dilute acid solution that must be added to obtain the desired pH. Then calculate the total amount of dilute acid that must be added to the entire system. Add small amounts of the acid solution at intervals, make sure it is quickly mixed with the system water and try to keep the fish away from the "hot zones" where the concentration of acid is temporarily high. Be careful with acids because they can cause severe injury. Wear protective clothing, rubber gloves, goggles and an approved respirator. Never add water to acid because it will spatter. Always add acid to water.

Adding acid to a fish production system is tricky and not the best approach. It would be better to stock more fish and add more feed to transform the system into a true aquaponic system where the pH goes down and only base is needed to stabilize the pH.

➢ Bacteria and nitrification

Question

I am a chemistry student at the Illinois Institute of Technology in Chicago, Illinois. I was investigating Aquaponics as a possible food source for rural and urban peoples living in third world countries. In looking through your website, I became a little confused at the mention of using bacteria that serve as bio-filters. Are these bacteria added to the Aquaponics system or do they occur naturally? If they do need to be added to the system, what type of bacteria? Are they self-sustaining or do they need to be replaced over time? I would very much appreciate it if you could shed some light on these questions.

Answer

The bacteria become established naturally and sustain themselves by using ammonia and nitrite, toxic waste products, as an energy source. Fish excrete waste nitrogen through their gills in the form of ammonia. A group of bacteria called Nitrosomonas transforms ammonia to nitrite. Another group of bacteria called Nitrobacter transforms nitrite to nitrate, which is relatively non-toxic. Together these groups of bacteria are referred to as nitrifying bacteria and the process of converting ammonia to nitrite and nitrite to nitrate is referred to as nitrification.

Nitrification destroys alkalinity, resulting in a decrease in pH. Without the constant addition of some base compound such as calcium hydroxide, pH will continually decline until it reaches 4.5, which indicates a high level of acidity. As pH goes below 6.0, nitrification stops and ammonia accumulates to very high concentrations. It is therefore very important to maintain pH at approximately 7.0 to promote nitrification and the removal of toxic metabolites. Effective nitrification also requires adequate levels of dissolved oxygen, low levels of organic matter and exposure to open areas and water currents so that dead bacteria can slough off and create space for young growing bacteria. The underside of hydroponic rafts is an ideal environment for nitrifying bacteria.

➤ Nutritional requirements for tomatoes

Question
I am doing a project on aquaponics and need some data/information on the specific nutritional requirements for tomatoes. I am looking for rate data, e.g. tomatoes need x amount of N and y amount of P per day, etc. Also, I need to know if all of the required nutrients for growing tomatoes are available in an aquaponic system.

Answer
In hydroponics the emphasis is not on how much nitrogen (N) and phosphorus (P) the plants require daily but rather on maintaining sufficient levels of nutrients in solution so that there will be no limitations. The daily uptake of nutrients by plants varies over the production cycle. When plants are young or old or if it is cloudy, they will use less nutrients compared to when they

are at the peak growth stage or it is sunny or the temperature is optimum. Therefore, maintain sufficient levels of nutrients for growth, and the plants will absorb what they want. Sometimes they absorb more nutrients than they need. This is called luxury consumption.

In hydroponic nutrient formulations, N levels range of 140 to 200 ppm (mg/liter) while P concentrations range from 30 to 60 ppm (mg/liter). These are the initial nutrient concentrations in the hydroponic formulation. As the nutrient solution is used, the initial nutrient levels will decline as plants utilize the nutrients for growth. Eventually nutrient levels will become too low for good growth. At this point, the solution is either discarded and a new solution prepared or it is reconstituted.

You can determine how much N and P a tomato plant used during a production cycle by collecting all the vegetative matter produced by a plant, including the roots, drying it, weighing it, grinding it, removing a well mixed subsample, digesting it in acid to convert all of the material to a know volume of liquid, analyzing the N and P concentrations in the liquid and calculating the mass in grams of N and P in the liquid, which is multiplied by the subsample factor to determine their mass (g) in the plant. Dividing this mass by the number of growing days will give the average uptake per day, but this is an academic exercise that is not relevant to production operations.

In aquaponics, adequate levels of N and P can be maintained using a good feeding rate ratio. A feeding rate ratio of 3.5 oz (100 g) of fish feed per m^2 of plant growing area per day is sufficient for good tomato growth. In aquaponics, nutrient levels may be only 10% of those in hydroponic formulations, but in aquaponic systems nutrients are being generated every day unlike hydroponic solutions where nutrient levels always decline.

➢ Algae vs. nutrients in raft system

Question

I just set up a backyard system for now. I got some tilapia and now am having a lot of algae growth in all the tanks. I don't know what to do. Also, I've heard a lot of conflicting info that the raft system doesn't grow good tomatoes or cucumbers because there is not enough nutrition in the water. I was also told it will only grow lettuce successfully. Is that true?

Answer

Algae (phytoplankton) is growing because your tanks are exposed to sunlight. We install an opaque canopy over our fish rearing tanks and our solids removal component. The hydroponic tanks are completely covered by rafts. Therefore, sunlight does not make direct contact with the water, and there is never any algal growth in our aquaponic systems.

We have successfully grown more than 30 types of vegetables aquaponically. Cucumbers grow well. Tomatoes are a bit problematic. We have produced large crops of tomatoes. However, sometimes tomatoes develop a problem called vascular wilt. They will grow rapidly and start setting fruit, but then some plants will suddenly wilt and eventually die. It appears that they are not getting water, and the reason is that bacteria grow in their vascular systems, blocking the uptake of water. There are tomato varieties that show resistance to vascular wilt, but we have not conducted a variety trial.

Plant nutrition is not a problem in aquaponic systems if you maintain a feeding rate ratio of 2.1 oz – 3.5 oz (60-100 g) of fish feed per square meter of plant growing area per day, supplement with calcium and potassium through base addition and add 2 ppm (mg/liter) of chelated iron every 3 weeks.

➢ Nitrate Level

Question

I have existing fish tanks and raise koi. We are adding some grow beds and rafts to four of our koi tanks. Before we setup a large growing system, we want to do some small scale units.

I have no trouble maintaining:

Ammonia at 0 to <.25 ppm (mg/liter)

Nitrite: 0 - <.25 ppm (mg/liter)

Nitrates: 80 to 160 ppm (mg/liter)

pH: 6.8 to 7.3

Alkalinity: 60 to 125 ppm (mg/liter)

The tanks vary, some have established bacteria and some were new start-ups. My question is what sustained nitrate level should I be looking for? I have started a few rafts with some aquatic plants we had in the greenhouse to help cycle out the nitrates. The aquatic mint and celery have taken off quite well. I have started some lettuce seeds, but it will be some time before they will be ready.

Answer

When you say that nitrates are in the range of 80 to 160 [mg/liter], you are most likely referring to the concentration of nitrogen that exists in the form of nitrate ions (NO_3^-). Plants absorb the majority of the nitrogen they need for growth as nitrate ions, but it is only the weight of the nitrogen in the nitrate ion that is used to express its concentration in mg/liter (mg/L) or parts per million (ppm), which are equivalent units. The correct symbol for designating the nitrate concentration is $NO_3\text{-}N$, which indicates that it is only the weight of the nitrogen in the nitrate ion that is being measured.

A wide range of nitrate-nitrogen concentrations are used in

140

hydroponic nutrient formulations. In general, nitrate-nitrogen concentrations range from 100 to 200 ppm (mg/liter). These are the starting concentrations that decrease as plants absorb nitrate ions. Aquaponic systems operate effectively at much lower nitrate-nitrogen concentrations because nitrate ions are being produced continuously through the process of nitrification, the oxidation of ammonia excreted by the fish to nitrite which in turn is converted to nitrate. Nitrate-nitrogen concentrations in aquaponic systems rarely exceed 80 ppm (mg/liter) and can go as low as 20 ppm (mg/liter) without causing adverse effects on plant growth. Lower values are recommended for fruiting plants to ensure good fruit set. If nitrate-nitrogen concentrations are too high, excessive vegetative growth will occur in fruiting plants to the detriment of fruit set.

Nitrate-nitrogen concentrations can be controlled through the process of denitrification, the reduction of nitrate to nitrogen gas, which is mediated by anaerobic bacteria that grow in the absence of oxygen. The majority of denitrification in the UVI system occurs in the filter tank where organic waste accumulates on orchard netting and forms anaerobic zones. Decreasing the cleaning frequency of the netting to once a week will increase denitrification and lower the nitrate-nitrogen levels in the system. Conversely, increasing the cleaning frequency to twice a week reduces denitrification and increases nitrate-nitrogen levels.

In practical terms, plants grow well over a wide range of nitrate-nitrogen levels, and in a well designed system the concentration of nitrate-nitrogen should not be a concern. However, if fruit set is poor or plants leaves become yellow (also a symptom of iron deficiency), determine the nitrate-nitrogen concentration to see if it is causing the problem.

➤ Nitrate absorption per square foot

Question

I have some questions and am wondering if you could help me with some calculations. I am currently experimenting with an aquaponic system using a small fish tank with tilapia which is connected to an ebb and flow tray/grow bed full of lettuce. The system is working well but in order to expand it I would like to know the amount of nitrate that is absorbed by the plants so I will have an understanding of the filtration capacity of the grow bed. This, therefore, affects the quality of water for the tilapia. It would be most helpful if you have average nitrate absorption levels per square ft of grow bed for a particular plant. Following this question is the other side of the equation, do you have calculations or figures on the average nitrate production per fish or per pound of fish in the tank?

Answer

I assume the ebb and flow tray contains some sort of media. At the University of the Virgin Islands we use a deep flow channel that remains full of water and is covered by a polystyrene raft, which supports the plants. I am at a loss in not knowing what media (aggregate) you have and what the specific surface area is. Specific surface area is the amount of surface area per unit volume of media. The specific surface area increases as the size of the media decreases. Surface area provides space for ammonia and nitrite removing bacteria to attach and grow, and with more surface area and bacteria more ammonia and nitrite will be removed. Ammonia production and removal rates depend on a large number of factors. It is estimated that 2.2 lbs (1 kg) of ammonia are produced for every 100 lbs (45.4 kg) of fish feed. The bacteria in your growing bed need to convert this ammonia to nitrite and then to nitrate. Since I do not know what media you have, I cannot comment on the amount of substrate you will need to convert all the ammonia and nitrite to nitrate. Ammonia and nitrite are toxic to the fish but nitrate is relatively non-toxic. However, nitrate does affect fish growth at very high concentrations (>500 ppm (mg/liter)). Plants absorb ammonia and nitrate and keep nitrate from accumulating. In recirculating aquaculture systems nitrate ions accumulate so fast that 5-10% of the system's water must be exchanged daily to remove excess nitrate. The removal of nitrate ions by plants in aquaponic systems prevents nitrate from accumulating and therefore water exchange rates are typically near 1%.

I am most familiar with the UVI aquaponic system, which employees raft hydroponics. The design of this system is based on the optimum feeding rate ratio for good plant growth, which ranges from 2.1 oz – 3.5 oz (60 to 100 g) of fish feed per square meter of plant growing area per day (60-100 g/m^2/day). At this feeding rate ratio plants have sufficient nutrients for growth, and nutrients remain at relatively constant levels for a wide variety of vegetables. Daily makeup water, which averages 1.5% of system volume, replaces water lost through sludge removal, splashing, evaporation and transpiration. The maximum feeding rate ratio for acceptable water quality in the UVI system is 180 g/m^2/day. Therefore, the system is designed to operate well within its capacity for water treatment.

Only once did we indirectly measure nitrogen removal in a production trial with a thick stand of romaine lettuce. Total nitrogen removal was 0.83 g/m^2 of plant growing /day. This rate was determined by measuring total nitrogen in the plants and dividing it by the number of days the plants were cultured in the system. We could not differentiate what portion of this removal was due to ammonia or nitrate update.

I always discourage the use of aggregates in commercial aquaponic systems because they can easily clog with organic matter and become a net generator of ammonia. However, at the hobby level, aquaponic systems with aggregate filled hydroponic beds work well and are small enough to be occasionally cleaned if they clog.

To answer your question from a broader perspective, what you need your growing beds to do is remove ammonia and nitrite to maintain good water quality for the fish. That is the prime consideration. Plants will remove some of the nitrate but generally not all of it. Much of the nitrate is removed by the process of denitrification, which is performed by bacteria growing in anaerobic (no oxygen) zones of your system, especially if you have an aggregate hydroponic substrate. If nitrate ions are still too high for good fruit development, the water exchange rate can be increased slightly to dilute the culture water and obtain desirable nutrient levels.

Aquatic Pests

> ## Ostracods in the raft tank

Question

We have a large-scale raft aquaponic system. We have a good coating of beneficial bacteria on the underside of the rafts and the ammonia and nitrite levels are low. You can feel and see the light brown coating of beneficial bacteria but, in addition, there is something that feels gritty. Do you know what this might be and if it is a problem?

Answer

I encountered this situation in the early stages of the development of the UVI system. It turned out that this gritty material consisted of small crustaceans known as ostracods, which are sometimes called seed shrimp. They are typically 1 mm (0.04 in) in size. Their flat bodies are protected by two hard calcareous shells connected by a hinge, which resembles the shell of a clam. There are thousands of species of ostracods, which are found in saltwater, freshwater and aquaponic systems if they are accidentally introduced. Their appendages allow them to hold onto plant roots and move quickly up and down the roots. They can be carnivores, herbivores, scavengers, or filter feeders.

The ostracod species that infested the UVI system harmed lettuce roots and reduced plant growth. At that time the 100 ft (30.5 m) hydroponic tanks contained air stones (diffusers) 8 ft (2.4 m) apart. The currents generated by the air bubbles appeared to dislodge the ostracods, and the plants grew normally. However, in the quiescent zones between the air stones, the ostracods flourished and lettuce growth was inhibited. When the hydroponic tank was viewed from the side, the profile of the plants resembled a wave, gradually increasing in height near the air stones and gradually decreasing in height near the quiescent zones. When the lettuce roots were viewed under a microscope, we could see the ostracods moving rapidly up and down the roots. At that time I hypothesized that they were affecting plant growth by either eating the root hairs or knocking them off incidentally, but I could not be sure of the exact mechanism of harm. We quantified the number of ostracods on one plant by shaking its roots vigorously in a large beaker of water and counting the ostracods in a subsample. We calculated that the roots of one lettuce plant contained 25,000 ostracods.

To solve the ostracod problem we doubled the number of air stones, spacing them 4 ft (1.2 m) apart, and added ornamental fish to the hydroponic tanks. We evaluated guppies, red swordtails and black high fin tetras, all of which eliminated the ostracods. We no longer use tropical fish, but the ostracods have never returned. Of these tropical fish I recommend using black high fin tetras or some other egg laying fish that will not overpopulate the hydroponic tanks. Livebearers such as guppies can multiply by the thousands, leading to the elimination of their food supply. As they search for food among the plant roots, they too can cause incidental damage to the plant roots.

If you use well water in an environmentally controlled greenhouse and buy sex-reversed fingerlings, the source of ostracods could be the water in the plastic bags containing the fingerlings. It is recommended that plastic bags containing fingerlings be floated in the receiving tank until the water temperatures equilibrate, and then slowly blend the waters and release the fingerlings. I suggest that the fingerlings be released into a large fine-meshed net which can be lifted out of the first receiving tank and moved to a second tank, in effect rinsing the fingerlings. The water in the first receiving tank should then be discarded.

➢ Midge fly

Question

We have something growing in our raft tank that looks like insect larvae of some sort. There are tiny reddish worms that emerge from the casings shown in this photo. I don't see them in the fish tanks, but maybe the fish eat them. Can you help me identify this? Is it harmful to my plants, fish or bacteria?

Answer

What you see are the chironomid larvae, the larvae of midges (non-biting gnats). The picture shows silt-covered tubes that protect the larvae during the day. At night they come out of the tubes to eat organic matter. The larvae hide inside the tubes because they are bright red in color and a favorite food for fish.

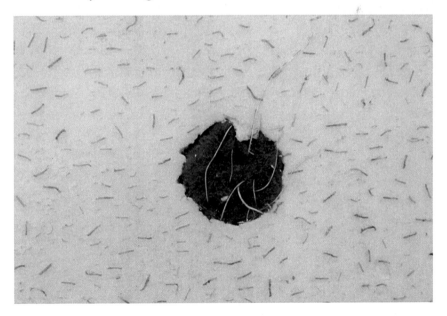

Midge fly larvae living on the underside of a polystyrene raft

Chironomid larvae grow in waters that are rich in organic matter. Their life cycle is a month long, going from egg to larva to pupa to adult. They are sometimes mistaken for mosquitoes, but they do not feed as adults. After pupating, adult midges emerge at sundown, gathering in swarms at water's edge or near lights and produce a humming sound that can be heard several feet away.

The underside of aquaponic rafts is an ideal growing site for chironomid larvae. Although they do eat nitrifying bacteria, I believe their density is generally not high enough to significantly impact the biofiltration capacity of the raft or harm the system. They confer a benefit to aquaponic systems by consuming organic matter, incorporating it into their bodies and then removing it from the system by flying away.

Chironomid larvae, also known as blood worms due to their bright red color, can attain high population densities in deep deposits of organic matter as long as there is sufficient oxygen in the water. If the aeration is turned off and oxygen levels decrease, the larvae leave their protective cases and can be captured with a net and used as fish feed. Frozen blood worms can be purchased and fed to valuable aquarium fish or the larval stages of valuable food fish. The emphasis is on 'valuable,' because blood worms are expensive, about $25 for a 2.2 lb (1 kg) frozen package.

Plant Pests and Disease

➤ Root rot, root death and *Pythium*

Question

With the plants roots submerged in water, how do you prevent root rot and other root disease? Is susceptibility to root rot a factor in choosing plants for an aquaponic system? If you do have root rot or plant disease, how do you control it?

Answer

Root rot is prevented by having adequate levels of dissolved oxygen (DO) throughout the entire root mass. In the UVI raft aquaponic system, there is a small air stone every 4 ft (1.2 m) in the hydroponic tanks to maintain DO levels at 5 ppm (mg/liter) or higher. Each 100 ft (30.5 m) hydroponic tank has a total of 24 air stones. Air stones not only oxygenate the water, they also create currents that deliver nutrients throughout the root mass. Without oxygen in the water, the roots will die. If water circulation is not good and anaerobic (no oxygen) zones form in the interior of the root mass, those roots will die although exterior roots will remain healthy. Obviously though, this is not good for maximum plant growth. Aerated rafts using deep channel flow with water depth of about 1 foot (0.3 m) generally do not exhibit root death from oxygen deficiency as long as the aquaponic system has a good solids removal component. If solid waste from the fish is allowed

149

to enter the hydroponic tanks, it will accumulate on plant roots and create anaerobic conditions and cause root death. Aquaponic systems that grow plants in narrow channels bathed by a thin film of nutrient-laden water, a method know as nutrient film technique (NFT), have a greater chance of solids partially blocking the water flow and creating anaerobic zones than systems using raft culture. Very good solid removal techniques are needed in NFT systems.

Root death can also be caused by plant pathogens, the most common of which is a fungus from the genus *Pythium*. There are about 20 species of *Pythium*, and they are the scourge of aquaponics and hydroponics. *Pythium* species have different water quality preferences, especially temperature, and some species kill roots at their optimum water temperature while others merely turn the roots tan and slow the plant's growth.

The best way to control *Pythium* is through temperature regulation or the selection of plants that exhibit natural resistance. For example, *Pythium* is not a problem in the UVI system in the winter when water temperatures are 75°F (23.9°C) or lower, but it does become a problem in the summer when water temperatures reach 84°F (28.9°C), especially with a crop like lettuce that prefers cooler conditions. However, crops such as okra, cantaloupe and endive resist *Pythium* when water temperatures are high.

Even with lettuce there are varieties that are more resistant than others. Although *Pythium* reduces lettuce production in the summer, survival and harvest size are still at acceptable levels. It is a good practice to periodically remove any accumulation of solids on the floor of the hydroponic tank because it can serve as a reservoir for *Pythium* spores. One major advantage of aquaponics is that it creates a balanced ecology with a diverse community of microbes, some of which are antagonistic to *Pythium* and keep it in check. In a sterile hydroponic system, an outbreak of *Pythium* can be devastating.

➤ Damping-off disease

Question

I set up a small aquaponic system with the grow bed on top of the fish tank. There is a 5 inch (12.7 cm) layer of perlite in the grow bed and I cycle the water through with a 170 gph water pump. I started the tank with 10 gold fish and let it run for 2 weeks. After 3 more weeks I sprinkled some flower seeds into the grow bed. They sprouted quickly. But, once they grew to about 2.5 inches (6.35 cm) tall, they fell over. They look healthy until they fall. I added some lettuce seeds and the same thing happens. I currently have 20 one inch (2.5 cm) gold fish. Do you have any idea what I am doing wrong? I have been adding about 1 gal of de-chlorinated water a week and I try to keep the ph at 6.5 to 7.

Answer

I think your problem is referred to as damping off disease in which fungi attack the tender young stems of your plants. Usually, in aquaponics, we do not plant seeds directly into the hydroponic substrate. Instead, we produce seedlings in a growing media such as coconut fiber (coir) where we can regulate the moisture level. If the media is too wet during this stage, damping off will occur. When the plant is older (about 3 weeks) and stronger (3 inches high), it is transplanted into the hydroponic substrate.

Another possibility in your system is that there may be some anaerobic (no oxygen) pockets in your perlite medium due to the accumulation of organic matter. I suggest that you use an intermittent pumping system that is run by a timer. During periods that the pump is off, the perlite will become saturated with air, ensuring that oxygen reaches all the plant roots. You will have to experiment to determine the best interval between pumping (flooding) and not pumping (draining). If the drain cycle (no pumping) is too long, there may not be enough aeration for the fish or enough water for the plants, causing them to wilt. Additionally, the perlite will not be working as a biofilter during drains cycles, leading to the accumulation of toxic metabolites (ammonia, nitrite) in the culture water. Therefore, the drain cycles should not be too long.

➤ Necrosis at base of plant stem

Question

We are working on aquaponics in the tropics in Saudi Arabia. Water from tilapia tanks flows into the channels covered by Styrofoam boards containing net pots with lettuce plants. The water then returns back to the tanks through a pump after about 2 hours retention in the channels. The growth of lettuce is very good. However, it is observed that about 20-35% plants are dying because of similar reason... necrosis (decaying) of the part of the stem which joins the root system with rest of the plant. Any guesses for the reason? Is it any pest, the larvae of which eat the particular portion of stem resulting in the breakage of the plant from the root system or something else?

Answer

We have experienced the same problem at the University of the Virgin Islands (UVI) from time to time. It is caused by a disease agent such as bacteria or fungi. Two genera of fungi (*Rhizoctonia* and *Phythium*) are associated with a damping-off disease where necrosis develops at the base of the stem and the plant suddenly dies. This usually occurs during the first week to 10 days after transplanting. To increase survival, the transplants must be removed very carefully from the seedling trays. Do not pull the plants out by the leaves as this can damage the stem and break roots, allowing an entry point for microbes. It is best to push the transplants out from the bottom of the tray using a peg board or the head of a large nail.

Before planting, the surface of the polystyrene sheets should be washed removing all plant debris and a circular brush should be run trough the planting holes to remove residue from the previous planting. Similarly, the net pots should be washed and soaked in a mild bleach solution to disinfect them. Make sure they are rinsed properly. Phosphorous acid (H_3PO_3), which is a nutrient and does not require regulation can be used to increase a plant's resistance to disease. Immerse the seedling tray in a 1% solution of H_3PO_3 the day before transplanting. Then spray lightly at weekly intervals with a 0.5% solution. Do this in the evening for better absorption and be careful not to apply too heavily as it can burn the leaves. Finally, create a small nursery area at double the normal density on some of the polystyrene sheets. Use the extra plants as replacement plants if some mortality occurs during the first 10 days. After 10 days, any unused replacement plants should be discarded as they become too large for transplanting.

If you can control water temperature in your system, lower it to 75°F (23.9°C). At that temperature lettuce grows optimally and is more resistant to *Pythium* infections. However, the growth rate of the tilapia will decrease slightly as tilapia prefer temperatures above 80°F (26.6°C).

NOTE: This system is based on the UVI design.

➢ Pest insects causing problems

Question

I am experiencing some problems with my aquaponic system (raft type). Some small black water bug is eating all our vegetables (bok choi, green lettuce). When these are almost gone, they are consuming roots of our cherry tomatoes. Most of these black water bug started appearing when my staff accidentally poured sludge from red-claw waste and fish feed remains into the vegetable bed. Initially, there was an algae bloom, followed by sudden increase in the black water bug population.

Diseased plants

Since they were eating algae from the vegetables bed, I thought it will be a good thing. I thought they are some kind of plankton, and would not harm any of the vegetables. But after a week, my healthy bok choi started dying. When I picked the bok choi up, I saw some of them were actually hiding in the rotting areas of the bok choi. That's when I realized they were attacking our vegetables. I added some small fishes to control their population, which did work for a while, but now they're hiding among vegetables roots, and attacking all vegetables roots as well. I really need your expertise on this. So far, my pH is slightly above 7. It was close to 8 because I initially added corals (to stabilize water pH) to my filter. But the pH dropped after I moved all my corals away from the vegetable bed. I'm currently trying to add phosphorus acid to the vegetables bed.

Answer

Your problem has me stumped. On one of the pictures you sent, I can see a small green insect that looks like an aphid or some sort of scale insect. Your plants are dying completely. It is possible that something else has weakened the plants, and the insects moved in as a result but did not actually initiate the problem. When plants are stressed, they lose their natural immunity and insects often take advantage. I am wondering if you had a record of success before this incident occurred. If not, it could be that there is something wrong with your source water or feed or nutrient levels. We never add phosphoric acid. I guess you may be doing that to lower pH. You should never let your pH reach 8.0 because nutrients will precipitate out of solution at this pH. Once your nitrifying bacteria have become established, the pH will decrease. It is important that it does so you can add calcium hydroxide and potassium hydroxide not only to maintain pH at 7.0 but to supplement calcium and potassium. Also remember that you need to supplement with a chelated iron compound every few weeks.

At this stage I recommend totally disinfecting your system, starting over with good water, and ensuring that your nutrient levels are adequate. And it goes without saying that red claw sludge should not be added to your system. Good luck.

Fish Feeds and Feeding

> ## Source of fish food; hand feeding vs. automatic

Question

There are quite a few fish food suppliers in the US. Do you have a preference on which food to buy? Do you prefer hand feeding or automatic feeders?

Answer

We have not conducted growth studies comparing different fish feed brands so I cannot recommend a particular fish feed supplier. We base our decision mainly on convenience and reliability because we must buy all of our feed

Pelletized fish food

from a feed shop in Miami and have it shipped to the Virgin Islands on a regular basis.

We do not prefer automatic feeders. We have tried belt feeders and demand feeders and found them both to have drawbacks for aquaponic systems. The belt feeders are mounted on the edge of the fish tanks. At the beginning of each day a conveyor belt is

Dr. Rakocy monitoring feeding behavior after hand feeding the fish

pulled across the bottom of a plastic tray and the day's feeding ration is placed on the belt. Feed falls off the belt into the fish tank through a gap in the tray as a spring wound clock mechanism slowly rolls the belt onto a shaft. We found that feed fines (small feed particles that break off the pellets) and water splashed by the fish would eventually gum up the spring mechanism. Returning the next morning we often found that none of the previous day's ration dropped into the tank.

Demand feeders allow the fish to feed themselves by triggering the release of feed when they hit a rod that hangs from the feeder into the rearing tank water. The demand feeder, which has a conical bottom, is mounted above the tank. The rod extends through a hole at the bottom of the cone. A plastic disc is attached to the rod just under the opening of the cone. There is a narrow gap between the disc and the cone. When the demand feeder is filled with feed, the disc prevents the feed from falling into the rearing tank water. The feed rests loosely on the disc. As the fish touch the rod, some of the feed pellets fall into the water, which leads to vigorous feeding activity, knocking more feed into the tank. When all the fish are sated, they stop hitting the rod, but they quickly learn that hitting the rod will provide a meal when they are hungry again.

We found three problems with demand feeders in our aquaponic system. Sometimes the feed clumped and blocked the narrow gap between the disc and the cone opening, which prevented feed from falling into the water regardless of how hard the fish hit the rod. [I guess the analogy here is putting your money in a vending machine and the desired candy bar doesn't drop out. Have you found yourself banging the machine?] If the aquaculturist is not paying attention the fish may go unfed. Another problem occurred because our systems are located outdoors, and the demand feeders were attached to the frame (hoops) of a partial greenhouse covered with a sheet of black plastic to shade the fish tanks. On a very windy day the structure shook so hard that feed was discharged without the fish hitting the rod. At the end of the day we sometimes found the tank covered with feed that would be wasted. Finally, we observed that the dominate males guarded the rod and would not let the smaller fish trigger the release of feed. This was what we experienced, but demand feeders work well in other situations. We obtained excellent results with home-made demand feeders mounted on top 1-m^3 cages in farm ponds. The feed we buy these days does not clump, and we have a better greenhouse structure. However, I do believe that in large tanks demand feeders are less effective.

There are other types of automatic feeders, but we prefer manual feeding three times daily to gauge the feeding response and assess the condition of the fish. We feed as much as the fish can consume in 30 minutes and adjust the amount of feed once or twice a week according to feeding response.

➢ What do you feed the fish?

Question

I have been to your website and I am interested in starting a small aquaponic system to grow food for my family and friends. Eventually, I would like a larger, commercial system. In the past, I have raised trout in ponds. My questions are about fish food. What do you feed the fish? Are there low-cost options? Do you feed a fish like a tilapia differently than a trout?

Answer

We feed tilapia a complete diet which contains 32% protein, 3% fat and a mineral and vitamin mix, which supplies all of the essential minerals and vitamins. It is a floating pellet so we can observe the feeding response and can feed *ad libitum*, an amount that the fish can consume in approximately 30 minutes. We feed three times daily.

Trout feed contains 38-45% protein and 10-18% fat. Sometimes even higher levels of protein and fat are used in trout feed. Trout feed also contains vitamin and mineral mixes to obtain a complete diet. Differences in the formulated diets reflect the differences in the natural food of these fish species. Tilapia is omnivorous and feeds low on the food chain, growing well on a diet of detritus, algae and bacteria while trout are predators, consuming other fish and insects, which are high in protein. I suggest buying commercially available feed for tilapia grown in an aquaponic system. Such a diet will produce a high growth rate and sufficient minerals required for good plant production.

➤ Duckweed, worms, fly larvae, etc

Question

I have read a lot about aquaponics and I am interested in setting up a sustainable system. One issue I have is with the pelleted tilapia food. I have read articles that mention feeding tilapia duck weed, worms, fly larvae, etc. Is this a viable option for commercial production and can it produce the same results as the commercially available fish food? Are there any natural or organic fish foods on the market? If so, how do they compare to non-natural feeds in relation to the weight gain of the fish? If not, are there fish food recipes available so that I could make my own with natural ingredients?

Answer

When you mention commercial aquaculture production, there is nothing that compares with commercial pelleted feed in 50 lb bags. At a modest commercial scale, say 100,000 lbs (4,536 kg) a year, you will be feeding about 400 to 450 lbs (181 – 204 kg) of feed per day (8 to 9 bags). It is not feasible to feed duckweed, worms, fly larvae, etc. at this level of production. You will spend more time gathering feed than raising fish, and the feed that you do gather will probably not be as nutritious as commercial feed, which is formulated to have the correct levels of protein, energy (carbohydrates and fat), vitamins and minerals.

The major ingredients in tilapia feed for example are corn and soybeans. We use 32% protein feed for best results. At a maximum about 5% of the protein comes from fish meal. Proponents of sustainable production object to the use of fish meal because natural supplies of fish in the oceans for making fish meal are running out. However, fish really do grow best when they receive some fish meal, which has the ideal mix of amino acids, the building blocks of fish flesh. The use of fish meal is one of the sticking points to receiving organic certification for fish feed because there is no control over the wild caught fish that go into fish meal. Some of these fish may contain traces of dangerous compounds.

To my knowledge there are currently no certified organic fish feeds on the market, although companies are working to develop certified organic fish feeds. When companies have used all plant protein sources for fish feed, the growth results have been disappointing. I do not think you can classify feed for fish as natural or non-natural. Corn, soybeans and fish meal are certainly natural products. Every feed will have vitamin and mineral mixes added to ensure proper growth. The vitamins are produced synthetically and the minerals are extracted from ore and processed to create pure forms.

There has been a huge amount of research on feed for aquaculture. For example, in the December issue of the Journal of the World Aquaculture Society there are 11 papers, seven of which deal with feed formulations. There are numerous recipes for making fish feed. However, I do not recommend that you make your own feed until you have become a major U.S. producer. In fact, even the major producers buy their fish feed. Millions of dollars have been spent on research to make the best feed possible. Manufacturing feed is a business of its own, and devoting time to it will distract you from growing and marketing fish. Believe me when I say that raising and marketing fish will require 100% of your time to be commercially successful.

Crop Choices

➢ Crop yields

Question

I'm working on a proposal for an aquaponic system and I'm looking for data on crop yields. Do you have any data that you could share on this?

Answer

The UVI aquaponic system is an outdoor system in a tropical climate. We have production data on three crops – lettuce, basil and okra. We intend to collect additional data on many other crops.

Using raft culture in a system with 2,304 ft^2 (214 m^2) of growing area, we have produced an average of 27 cases of leaf lettuce per week over a 3 year period. Production was staggered and the culture period in the system was 4 weeks. Annual production averaged 1,400 cases of leaf lettuce with 24-30 heads of lettuce per case. The maximum potential harvest per week was 36 cases. The marketable harvest was 75% of the maximum possible harvest. The 25% loss was due to disease, insect damage or small head size, which required adding more heads of lettuce to a box than the standard 24 heads. This data is very realistic. You should never assume that every plant will be marketable quality.

An experiment with sweet basil showed that the UVI system can produce an average of 11,000 lbs (4,990 kg) annually, which is equivalent to 4.77 lbs/ft^2. Production was staggered, and the culture period was 8 weeks. Stems were harvested (cut) after 4

In batch culture, okra production trials resulted in 2.73 lbs/ft²

weeks of growth and allowed to re-grow for another 4 weeks before the final harvest.

Finally, an experiment with okra showed that annual production was 6,300 lbs (2,858 kg) of okra pods, which is equivalent to 2.73 lbs/ft². The okra was produced by batch culture. The entire system was planted at the same time. After 4 weeks the plants flowed, and, commencing during the 5th week, harvests took place every other day up to 12 weeks when the crop declined due to mildew. Three or four plantings would be required annually.

➤ List of crops that have been grown at UVI

Question

I am writing a report for my 11ᵗʰ grade agri-science class on aquaponics and I am looking for information on what crops can be grown. Can you provide me a list of crops that have been grown at the University of the Virgin Islands and also tell me which ones have been most successful and why?

Answer

We have grown many crops, but we have not tested all of the potential crops that can be grown in an aquaponic system and we have only scratched the surface in evaluating the production levels of crops in a raft aquaponic system. The crops we have grown include lettuce (50 varieties), Swiss chard, endive, radicchio, spinach, water spinach, amaranth, arugula, celery, parsley, pak choi, tatsoi, Chinese cabbage, collard, kale, mustard, basil (many varieties), mint (many varieties), garlic chives, common chives, dill, cilantro, recao, okra, tomato, cherry tomato, yellow squash, zucchini, cucumber, watermelon, cantaloupe, bell pepper, hot pepper, pole bean, eggplant, peas, beets, rice, nasturtium, zinnia and marigold.

The crops I highly recommend are lettuce, basil and mint because they grow fast, have few insect or disease problems and are very profitable. Leafy green plants and herbs in general are recommended. The plants of these groups that did not perform well included radicchio, spinach, arugula and celery. It was too warm here for radicchio to produce a compact head. Spinach did not grow well. Mortality was high for arugula during the establishment stage. The plants that became established grew well. Celery did not form a compact head.

The fruiting plants grow well, but they are more prone to insect problems and disease because of their long growth cycle. It takes these plants a relatively long time to bear fruit, and therefore they are not as profitable as the rapid-growing leafy green plants and culinary herbs, some of which (e.g., basil) are nearly 10 times more profitable than fruiting plants. If the goal is to use aquaponics as a backyard garden, then fruiting plants are an essential component. An aquaponic system with a mixture of 10 to 20 vegetables can replace the backyard garden as a source of fresh produce for the family diet.

Beets are grown for their purple leaves, which are added to salads. Rice, a wetland grain, grows well, but it is not economical. Nasturtium, an edible flower that is added to salads, grows well. Zinnia and marigolds grow very well in aquaponic systems. There are so many other flowers that need to be tested. Like a garden, a backyard aquaponic system can be a source of fresh flowers for the house. Aquaponic systems can be brought right into the house in a southern-facing sunroom for year-round production of fish, vegetables and flowers.

➤ Salt tolerant crops

Question
What kind of marketable plant tolerates brackish water with salinities of 10-14 ppt and can be grown in aquaponics? I am trying to design a prawn hatchery using aquaponics as a base and must find out how the effluent from the larvae tanks could provide nourishment to plants. Kelp is a strong candidate at this time. However, there might be other plants suitable for brackish water which could also be commercially viable.

Answer
There are two types of plants that can be grown in saline aquaculture effluent. One type is the seaweed, *Ulva* spp. and

Gracilaria spp., which are being cultured in mariculture systems in Israel. The world's leading expert on this technology is Dr. Amir Neori. These plants are grown submerged in effluent ponds or raceways to remove nutrients and produce a byproduct with significant commercial value. The technology for raising these plants is quite different than a standard aquaponic system. The water must be deeper, and the water treatment capacity of these plants will be different. Another factor to consider is their salinity requirement. I am not sure how well these plants do in brackish water as opposed to full strength salt water. There are probably species differences in regards to optimum salinity. I suggest you study Dr. Neori's publications, some of which can be accessed through Google.com.

The other potential plant candidate for your system is *Salicornia*, a genus of succulent, salt tolerant plants that grow in salt marshes, on beaches and among mangroves. Some common names for *Salicornia* are glasswort, pickleweed and march samphire. *Salicornia* is a succulent herb. The species *Salicornia europaea* is highly edible either cooked or raw. It is generally steamed or microwaved and coated with butter. In the United States the edible species are known as sea beans. *Salicornia* is a short plant, approximately 1 ft (0.3 m) tall, with roots that could be grown using polystyrene sheets. However, I am not aware if anyone has attempted to grow it in an aquaponic system.

> ### Tomatoes, cantaloupe

Question

I have read references to the UVI system growing vegetables like tomatoes and cantaloupe but I didn't think these could be grown successfully in aquaponics. What kind of results have you had? Do you recommend these crops? Do you need more fish (and fish waste) in the system to grow tomatoes rather than lettuce? Are there issues in growing these crops in aquaponics in my climate (Ontario)?

Answer

Yes, you can raise tomatoes and cantaloupe in aquaponic systems using the high end of the range for feeding rate ratios (100 g/m^2/day). In your climate you will need supplemental lighting in the winter. A long time ago we raised four varieties of tomatoes for 16 weeks in a gravel aquaponic system. We obtained yields as high as 22 lbs (10 kg) per plant and 3.7 lb/ft^2 of growing space. Since this research was performed 22 years ago, the varieties are probably no longer in existence. In our outdoor system we found that determinate tomatoes performed best. Determinate tomatoes grow like a bush, and all the fruit is set at the same time similar to the garden variety of tomato.

Recently we have grown tomatoes for demonstration in our commercial-scale aquaponic system with mixed results. The tomatoes often do well until small fruits develop, but then the plant will wilt and die. Wilting is caused by the blockage of the plant's vascular system (xylem for transporting water and phloem for transporting sugar) by bacteria. There has been considerable research on this problem, which affects soil-grown tomatoes too, and there are varieties of tomatoes available that show resistance to wilt. We have not pursued aquaponic tomato production because tomatoes are not nearly as profitable as the production of culinary herbs and lettuce in aquaponic systems.

Cantaloupe thrives in our commercial-scale aquaponic system and reaches remarkable sizes. We have harvested some cantaloupe weighing as much as 11 lbs (5 kg). Cantaloupe is a 90-day crop, but when the production cycle is over our hydroponic beds are full of large cantaloupe. The problem is that cantaloupe grown in water is not as sweet as cantaloupe grown in soil. This is another crop that we have not pursued as much as we should because there are undoubtedly differences in sweetness between varieties, but too much water appears to affect sweetness. I have an idea that has not been tested. I wonder if sweetness can be induced by removing most of the roots as the crop approaches maturity. This would be easy to do with a raft system by just raising the polystyrene sheets and trimming the roots.

➤ Rice and grain

Question

I've recently seen references to aquaponics in the news and on blogs and I've done a lot of reading online about it. I find this technology fascinating and I'd like to know what you think the best uses of this technology are. Do you think there is potential in the future to grow any grain crops in aquaponics? If you could raise fish for protein, fresh vegetables and a grain, this one system would provide a nearly complete diet (less dairy).

Answer

I believe that aquaponics would work well with wetland rice cultivation. Fields could be arranged with a divider (a soil berm) so that effluent from the rearing tanks are discharged on one side of the berm and retuned on the other side similar to the UVI hydroponic tank array. A small gap at the far end of the berm would allow water to pass from the inlet side to the outlet side of the field. We have tested rice in our aquaponic system and it grows very well. Tilapia are grown in rice paddies in Southeast Asia, but stocking rates and growth rates are very low because the tilapia are not fed. They must forage for food. However, a system that involves intensive tank culture of fed tilapia and nutrient removal and water treatment by wetland rice could be very productive.

Growing other staples such as wheat, soybean or corn would require considerable experimentation, system design modifications and vision, but their cultivation in an aquaponic system may be possible.

Question

I am planning an Aquaponic setup for a sustainable cluster development project in Zimbabwe and am trying to find out if anyone has recently successfully cultivated maize or rice in a commercial aquaponics system. I know that the Vietnamese have had some luck with rice in open aquaponic systems but have not found any information on specifics of cultivation. Likewise, I am aware the Aztecs cultivated maize in an early aquaponic setup. Has anyone done this more recently?

The original plan was to cultivate the main food crops to sustain the cluster, i.e. tilapia, rape, maize or rice, beans, tomatoes and potatoes. The problem is the starch crop. Maize is the local staple so that is what I really want to produce.

Answer

Usually aquaponic systems are designed for high value crops such as culinary herbs and lettuce because the systems are expensive to build and operate. You are planning to produce lower value staple food items (rice, beans, corn) in a country that probably cannot afford to build or operate a standard aquaponic system. A standard system contains fish rearing tanks, a solids removal component (more tanks), hydroponic troughs, pumps and aerators. High quality feed is used to maximize fish production, which justifies the high capital and operating costs.

Let me suggest a different strategy. Use the aquaponic system to produce high value crops, such as tomatoes, lettuce and herbs, and use the solid waste to irrigate and fertilize field crops (rape, rice, beans, corn and potatoes). Build the system as inexpensively as possible. Use Ferro cement for tank construction. Use an

170

alternative covering to polystyrene sheets for the hydroponic rafts. Maybe bury all the tanks so you can use air lift pumps to move water. Finally you might have to use an alternative source of feed instead of high quality pelleted feeds. One possibility, which is often discussed for tilapia culture, is the use of duckweed, a small, rapidly growing plant that is high in protein. Duckweed can be grown in small natural water bodies that are fertilized with animal manures. I am not sure if the system you want for Zimbabwe is out there yet, but it will be developed in time because the need for alternative food production systems in developing countries is great.

➢ Edamame vegetable soybeans

Question

I plan to start a small "backyard" operation next spring to get a "hands on" learning experience in aquaponics. I am interested in growing edamame vegetable soybeans to market as whole plants to a fresh market. I thought about growing them in a float bed system, using Styrofoam to support the soybean plants in plastic web baskets. This way I can harvest the whole plant with the roots so the bean pods will stay fresh longer, plus I will not have all the dirt to remove like I would have if grown outside in the soil. Do you think this idea would work? Do you have any recommendations for success with my aquaponics project?

Answer

Although I have not raised soybeans in an aquaponic system, I am confident they will grow well in a float system. At UVI we have had good success with pole beans. In a demonstration with just a few plants, production was remarkable over a long period of time. I suggest starting the soybeans in trays and transplanting them into 2 inch (5 cm) net pots when they reach a few inches in height. You may have to experiment with planting density. I suggest starting with a density similar to that of leaf lettuce – 48 plants per sheet of polystyrene measuring 8 ft x 4 ft (2.4 m x 1.2 m). In subsequent trials you can adjust the density on new sheets based on your observations.

Thank you for suggesting soybeans as an aquaponic plant. I will also start some trials here at UVI to evaluate this potential new crop.

➤ Basil and mint

Question

My biology class at school is going to build an aquaponic system as a part of our botany study. I was assigned to research what plant types would be best. We are interested in basil or mint because they seem most interesting and I've read that they would be successful. What tips can you provide me about growing either of these? What are the drawbacks and benefits? What additional information on those plants and their requirements should we acquire?

Answer

You have selected two crops that are ideally suited for aquaponic systems. In fact, they grow like weeds, only they have high economic value. Bioshelters in Amherst, Massachusetts, has been growing basil successfully for 15 years and supplying outlets within a radius of 100 miles (161 km), including the Boston market. They use nutrient film technique and start about six to eight plants from seed in a rockwool cube. They harvest the entire cube when the plants reach the desired height.

Last year at UVI we conducted research on basil in our raft system and compared a batch culture method to a staggered cropping method. With batch culture the entire system is planted at one time and harvested 4 weeks later at the same time. In staggered production, plants in four stages of growth are cultivated simultaneously and every week one fourth of the plants are harvested. Individual 3-week old basil transplants, grown in coconut fiber (coir), were transferred to 2 inch (5 cm) net pots. The plants were sprayed twice a week with BT (a bacteria) to control caterpillars. The system was supplemented with potassium, calcium and iron. At harvest the plants were cut at a height 6 inches (15 cm) and allowed to re-grow. Our planting density was 8 plants/m^2, but a subsequent literature review revealed that the planting density could have been three times higher. Our results showed that staggered production was better than batch culture. With batch culture the demand for nutrients exceeded the system's capacity to generate nutrients and by the fourth harvest plants were displaying symptoms of nutrient deficiency which made them unmarketable. When we switched to staggered production, high nutrient demand in the final growth stages was counterbalanced by lower nutrient demand in the initial growth stages, thereby moderating the uptake of nutrients. We found that basil requires a higher feeding ratio than lettuce. Aquaponic systems should be designed to supply 100 g of feed per day per square meter of plant growing area when basil is cultured.

With staggered production our annual yield would have been 4.78 lbs/ft^2. Therefore, annual production from the entire system, which contains 2304 ft^2 (214 m^2) of plant growing space, would have been 11,013 lbs (4996 kg) including stem weight. In the Virgin Islands fresh basil with stems sells for $10/lb at a minimum. Total annual income from basil was therefore projected to be $110,131. Unfortunately, we cannot sell this much basil in the Virgin Islands. The market is not large enough. If we could sell it all I would be growing basil for a living.

As for mint, I do not have any quantitative data but we have tried it using a raft system and net pots. It thrives on the high nitrogen levels found in aquaponic effluent. I expect that it would be as lucrative as basil. Both mint and basil usually retail for $1.00/oz ($16.00/lb) in retail stores.

A possible drawback is the relatively short shelf live for fresh basil. Therefore, it must be harvested frequently in quantities that can be sold quickly. You will experience mainly benefits (high productivity, good income) with these crops.

➤ Basil nutrient requirements

Question

Can you supply me with guidelines as to the concentrations of the following nutrients required for the production of sweet basil or even general guidelines for: Ca, Mg, Na, K, PO$_4$, N (NO$_2$,NO$_3$,NH$_3$) S, Cu, Zn, B, Fe, Mg, Mo?

Answer

Sweet basil is one of the easiest plants to grow in an aquaponic system. Basil can tolerate a wide range of nutrient levels. The largest commercial aquaponic facility in the U.S., Bioshelters in Amherst, Massachusetts, has been growing basil commercially for nearly 15 years in a tilapia production system. I believe they are producing approximately 600 cases of basil leaves weekly. At the University of the Virgin Islands (UVI) we have been growing basil on and off for a long period of time under a variety of conditions. Our general guideline is to feed the fish at a ratio of 57 g per square meter of plant growing area per day. This ratio provides the good nutrient levels. We supplement with equal amounts calcium hydroxide and potassium hydroxide to maintain pH near 7.0. Every 3 weeks we add 2 ppm (mg/liter) of iron in the form of a chelated compound. In a commercial-scale aquaponic system at UVI that was used to produce lettuce continuously for 2.5 years, nutrient concentrations varied within the following ranges (mg/L), ranges that would have produced excellent sweet basil growth:

Ca: 10.7-82.1
Mg: 0.7-12.9
K: 0.3-192.1
NO_3^-N: 0.4-82.2
PO_4^-P: 0.4-15.3
SO_4^-S 0.1-23.0
Fe: 0.13-4.3
Mn: 0.01-0.19
Cu: 0.01-0.11
Zn: 0.11-0.80
B: 0.01-0.23
Mo: 0.00-0.17

Total ammonia-nitrogen and nitrite-nitrogen averaged 1.47 ppm (mg/liter) and 0.52 ppm (mg/liter) in the rearing tanks, respectively. The lower values represent the period during the beginning of the trial before nutrients displayed any substantial accumulation. Based on information I pieced together for Bioshelters, their ratio of feeding to plant growing area is approximately 3 lb (1400 g) per square meter per day. This figure may be off somewhat but the ratio employed by Bioshelters is, nevertheless, much higher. However, there are big differences between our systems. We remove sludge (organic solids) from the system very slowly (up to 1 week) so that it mineralizes, releasing in dissolved form many of the nutrients tied up in organic compounds.

Bioshelters removes particulate organic waste very rapidly (in just a matter of minutes) from their system. We use soft rainwater while Bioshelters uses hard well water. They also supplement with

175

calcium in the form of a base but have sufficient potassium in their well water. They must apply iron as a foliar spray and sometimes the plants display phosphorous deficiency (elongation). I have contrasted our two systems to illustrate the wide range in growing conditions under which sweet basil will thrive. Of course sweet basil would do well with any type of standard hydroponic nutrient formula but, hopefully, you plan to get most of your nutrients for free using aquaculture effluent.

➢ Watercress

Question

I wish to recirculate water from a mini fish farm through a grow bed to produce edible plants. Do you have any information on growing watercress in aquaponics? It is a favorite of mine.

Answer

Watercress grows luxuriantly in aquaponic systems. I have experience raising watercress in an aquaponic system that I developed at Auburn University in Alabama where I did my Ph.D. research. The system was established using existing concrete tanks, but the water in these tanks, at 30 inches (76 cm) was too deep to support watercress. Therefore, I supported the watercress on a sheet of aluminum window screen suspended horizontally about 4 inches (10 cm) below the water surface. Only 35 ft^2 (3.3 m^2) of space per system (there were three systems) was devoted to watercress because I was raising many other plants. A few sprigs of watercress were planted on May 21 and all the plants were harvested on October 11. Average production was 17.4 lbs (17.9 kg) per system. I'm sure I could have done much better if I had done partial harvests during the summer to create additional growing space as the plants quickly filled the available area.

Howard Resh describes an ingenious system for raising watercress in an outdoor hydroponic system using a nutrient film technique (Hydroponic Food Production, Fifth Edition, pages 224-234). This system could be adapted for aquaponics. Hydroponic beds 9 ft x 500-600 ft (2.7 m x 152.4-183 m) were constructed with black polyethylene liner (6 mil) in a leveled field with a slight slope lengthwise of 1 ft (0.3 m). A flow-through system was used, but nutrients were injected periodically at points along the length of the bed. Continuous use of nutrient solution was not economically feasible. After effective solids removal and good aeration, fish culture effluent could be used in place of a hydroponic nutrient solution. Effluent should be discharged into the bed at 100-ft. intervals to obtain better distribution of nutrients. The effluent should collect in a sump at the end of the beds and be pumped back to the fish component.

In the Resh system, a 1/8-inch thick, 100% polyester matting was placed on the bottom of the bed to provide root anchorage and facilitate lateral distribution of the water. Water pooled (1-2 inches (2.5-5 cm) deep) in the lower sections of the bed and, therefore, nursery weed matting was sufficient for root anchorage and lateral water distribution. Watercress seeds were started in beds containing a 1-inch layer of pea gravel. They were irrigated with an overhead sprinkler. Three-inch transplants were obtained in 6 weeks after germination. During the summer growing season, it took 3-4 weeks from transplanting to harvest, while in winter more than 6 weeks were needed to produce marketable plants. In the warm season, size uniformity at harvest was better with new plants. Therefore, the entire plant was removed, the mats were cleaned and new transplants were started after each crop. In the cool season, a single planting was harvested four to five times using a cutting and re-growth technique. Normal production averaged 12 bundles per linear foot of bed.

➢ Iceberg lettuce

Question

Can I grow iceberg lettuce and tropical vegetables in an aquaponic system? I live near the southern tip of Florida and would like to know if the warm temperatures and high humidity we have here will be factors in an aquaponic system.

Answer

You will have to consider temperature. Iceberg lettuce (head lettuce) will not grow well in the heat of a Florida summer. A solid head will not develop and often the core of the lettuce will start to rot before it is harvested. In the Virgin Islands we can raise head lettuce (Montello) during January and February. Your production period for head lettuce would be a month or two longer. However, raising head lettuce should not be your goal when there are other lettuces (red leaf, green leaf, Bibb and romaine) that are more nutritious and often command higher prices. Red and green leaf lettuces and Bibb lettuce can be raised under summertime conditions. You'll have to experiment as to which varieties do best in your system under your particular climatic conditions. There are 2,000 lettuce varieties, so you have your work cut out. However, you will be limited to a few dozen varieties that can be readily obtained from catalogs. We have good luck with Sierra (red leaf), Nevada (green leaf), Jericho (romaine, a heat tolerant variety) and Ostinata (Bibb). We can raise these lettuces during the heat of summer in the Virgin Islands, but our relative humidity (about 70% in the day and 90% at night) might be lower which can make a difference. High relative humidity reduces transpiration which is a mechanism for moving water and dissolved nutrients from the roots to the growing areas of the plant. High solar radiation and high air temperature induce rapid growth, but the nutrients required to support this growth in lettuce are not present

178

in sufficient quantities if the relative humidity is too high. This causes death in new cells which turn black, a condition known as tip burn. Some lettuce varieties are more resistant to tip burn than others.

Many vegetables can be raised in aquaponic systems at high summer temperatures. In the Virgin Islands, temperatures are in the mid-90s (35°C) every day during summer. Yet we have had excellent results at those temperatures with basil, okra, cucumber, cantaloupe, hot peppers and watermelon. You can approach aquaponics from a traditional farming perspective and alternate crops based on the season.

The preferred water temperature for many vegetables such as lettuce and tomatoes is around 70°F (21.1°C). In hydroponic and aquaponic systems, water temperature is generally more important to plant growth and health than air temperature. In environmentally controlled greenhouses, chillers are often used to lower water temperatures in addition to other systems (e.g., cooling pads) that are used to moderate air temperatures.

➢ Strawberries

Question

I'd like to know if strawberries would work well as a crop for an aquaponic system and, if so, would tilapia be most compatible or could I try bass or perch in the fish tanks? Any info you could provide will be appreciated.

Answer

Strawberries are raised hydroponically and they could be raised using nutrients from fish as opposed to inorganic nutrient formulations. However, culturing strawberries hydroponically is more complex than many other crops and using aquaculture effluent, which contains organic matter in addition to inorganic nutrients, would add another level of complexity. Let me explain.

First, there are three categories of strawberries: short-day types, day-neutral types and long-day types. Short-day types flower when it receives less than 12 hours of daylight, which occurs during autumn and winter. Day-neutral types flower irrespective of day length, while long day types flower in the summer when days are long. Fruits become mature about 6 weeks after flowering.

Strawberries need to have a chilling period for optimum production. Strawberries obtained in the spring should be planted immediately for a summer crop. For an autumn and winter crop in a heated greenhouse, obtain day-neutral plants in late spring and chill in a refrigerator for 3 to 4 months before planting. Strawberries grow best at temperatures from 64°-77°F (17-25°C), and temperatures should not go above 86°F (30°C). Temperatures from 64°-77°F (17-25°C) are suitable for bass and perch while tilapia prefer temperatures above 80° F (26.6°C).

Strawberries are very prone to fungal diseases. Therefore, there should be good air movement around the leaves to reduce humidity, and the surface of the growing media should remain dry. The main stem of the strawberry plant, which is called the "crown," is very prone to fungal attack if it becomes waterlogged. Therefore, the crown is planted three-quarters above a well-drained media. The roots will grow downward to contact the water. An NFT system is suitable as long as the crowns do not slip below the level of the gully. Other media often employed include gravel, expanded clay, vermiculite and perlite. These media should be irrigated from the bottom to ensure that the surface remains dry. Methods of water delivery include a flood and drain system or a small constant flow of water along the bottom of a gully. Fine media creates a potential problem with aquaculture effluent because it can clog with particulate organic matter or biological growth, which is stimulated by dissolved organic matter and inorganic nutrients. Good solids removal and pretreatment with a biological filter would prolong media use before it may have to be cleaned.

The nutrients in aquaponic systems are suitable for strawberries. Strawberries require high levels of potassium. Potassium and calcium are generally supplemented in aquaponic systems through the addition of equal amounts of potassium hydroxide and calcium hydroxide bases to neutralize the acid that is produced during nitrification (the oxidation of ammonia to nitrite then to nitrate). When strawberries are cultivated, more potassium hydroxide should be added than calcium hydroxide to maintain pH in the range of 7.0 to 7.5.

Question

Do you have any information on commercial aquaponic strawberry production?

Answer

I am not aware of commercial aquaponic strawberry production. However, strawberries are raised hydroponically and could be raised aquaponically if suitable conditions are provided. Please refer to a previous Aquaponics Journal Q and A (Volume VII, No.1, 2003), in which I answered a question pertaining to strawberry production. Also Tim Carpenter wrote an excellent article on hydroponic strawberry production in a 2002 edition of Aquaponics Journal (Volume VI, No. 4).

➢ Flowers

Question

From what I have read Nitrogen (N) is the predominant nutrient produced from broken down fish waste. I would like to utilize an aquaponic system to support some of my flowers like passion fruit. Can I just add an organic bloom supplement to my fish tank to make up for the lack of Phosphorous (P) and Potassium (K)?

Do you know of good flowering supplements that are not toxic to the fish and also keep the water from turning too dark. I still enjoy looking at my fish.

Answer

We have grown flowers successfully in the UVI system without any changes to operating procedures. There is sufficient phosphorus (P), and potassium (K) is always supplemented by adding potassium hydroxide (KOH) to maintain pH at 7.0.

The system water develops the color of tea due to the presence

Zinnias grown in the UVI raft system

of tannic acid and other organic compounds that are resistant to bacterial decomposition. These compounds are mild antibiotics which confer benefits to the system such as making the fish and plants more resistant to disease.

You might prefer to see your fish, but food-fish do not necessarily prefer to see you. Cultured food-fish are still wild and prefer to remain out of sight where they feel secure. However, you can remove the color by using ozone in a separate mixing chamber, through which a small side stream of water flows from the aquaponic system. The use of ozone is complicated, expensive and dangerous. A small ozone generator is needed. Just the right amount of ozone must be added to the water so that it dissipates before the water returns to the culture system because ozone is highly toxic to fish and plants. Ozone gas is also toxic to humans and so the area containing the ozone unit must be well ventilated. Ozone is used in very intensive recirculating systems to reduce levels of dissolved organic matter or as a disinfectant, but its use requires expertise and careful monitoring.

➤ Arugula

Question

I am able to routinely grow beautiful Manoa lettuce in my aquaponics system in Hawaii. My family (actually my 77 year old mother) loves arugula. I have tried on several occasions to grow the tasty leaves with little success. I have seen by searching the internet that arugula has a copper requirement. Please inform me of your knowledge and experience of arugula. My system is stocked with Chinese catfish and has an adequate supply of nitrate. Being a closed system, the pH can get down in the 6's. Perhaps arugula needs a higher pH?

Answer

In the UVI raft system we have experienced high mortality of arugula during the transplanting phase. It is a delicate plant that cannot tolerate transplanting shock. However, if it can survive transplanting, it grows well. I suggest you experiment with different seedling media and transplanting techniques. I recommend using a mixture of coconut fiber and vermiculate as media and being extremely careful in not breaking any roots during transplanting. Arugula grows well in a pH range of 6.0 to 7.0. I suggest keeping the pH near 7.0 to promote good nitrification, removal of ammonia and nitrite by bacteria.

Tilapia

> ➢ **Tilapia and Omega-3**

Question

I have been doing research on the internet and was somewhat dismayed by a Wikipedia, AAAS report that, according to a Wake Forest Study, Tilapia is not only low in Omega-3 but also high in Omega-6 which have the potential to increase the body's inflammatory response. Omega-6 have negative implications for many chronic diseases including heart disease. Since it appears that Tilapia is the most viable fish species variety for aquaponic farming, I wonder if anyone there has more information about the Omega-6 content study. I've seen that Perch (Jade and Yellow) are high in the Omega-3 and are a preferred fish by chefs. Has anyone conducted scientific (health impact) research comparing Tilapia with Perch? Is there anyone in this country producing any other fish variety commercially utilizing an aquaponic system?

Answer

You bring up a topic that has caused a whole lot of consternation among the public. The Wake Forest Study did show that tilapia and catfish have more omega 6 fatty acids than omega-3 fatty acids. Omega-3 fatty acids are anti-inflammatory and are thought to protect against heart disease, while omega-6 fatty acids are pro-inflammatory and are generally thought to be bad for heart health. Health experts recommend that we include more fish in our diet, but the study shows that not all fish are equal in their fatty acid composition. Cold water wild fish such as salmon and sardines have much higher levels of omega-3 fatty acids than fish such as tuna, grouper and snapper. Catfish and tilapia, which are two of most popular fish consumed in the US, not only have more omega-6 fatty acids than omega-3 fatty acids but they also have a particularly inflammatory omega-6 called arachidonic acid, which is probably due to the vegetable-oil enriched diet fed to farmed fish. Some of the tilapia sampled for this particular study contained more arachidonic acid and less omega-3 fatty acid than bacon or hamburger. This led the researchers to make the controversial statement that "the inflammatory potential of hamburger or pork bacon is lower than the average serving of farmed tilapia." Of course when the newspapers picked up on this study the headlines screamed that tilapia is worse for you than hamburger and bacon. That's when doctors and nutritionists jumped in and said, "Wait a second."

An international coalition of 16 dietary fats experts wrote that "replacing tilapia or catfish with hamburgers and bacon is absolutely not recommended." They said that omega-6 fatty acids are also found in vegetable oils, nuts, whole-wheat bread and chicken and are part of a healthy diet. They went on the say that tilapia and catfish are better choices than most other meat alternatives. They said that fish like tilapia are low in total and saturated fat, high in good quality protein, and are clearly part of a healthy diet. Conversely, though bacon may have lower omega-6 fatty acids, it has more fat, calories and salt. Excessive calories in a diet can cause fat deposition which leads directly to inflammation.

I believe the consensus among nutritionists and health experts is to take daily fish oil supplements to ensure that your omega-3 intake, specifically the EPA (eicosapentaenoic acid) and DHA (docosahexaenoic acid) components of fish oil, is sufficient to create a better balance with omega-6 fatty acids. Not only will this regimen help protect vascular health, but there is evidence to suggest that it is anticarcinogenic.

Australia's jade perch has extremely high levels of omega-3 fatty acids, more than salmon. The silver perch from Australia also has high levels of omega-3 fatty acids, but not as much as the jade perch. Both of these fish species are being cultured aquaponically in Australia in hobby systems. Australia does not have tilapia, and it is illegal to bring tilapia into the country. But don't feel sorry for Australia because it is blessed with many excellent fish species (Murray cod, barramundi, eels, jade perch, silver perch and golden perch) that are being cultured in recirculating aquaculture systems.

➤ What is the best species of tilapia?

Question

What is the best strain of tilapia for aquaponics? There appears to be a lot of different species and hybrids out there.

Answer

All tilapia species will do well in an aquaponic system. However, there are inherent differences among tilapia species and strains in regards to growth rate and tolerance to low water temperature and poor water quality that will be manifested irrespective of the culture system. In general, Nile tilapia (*Oreochromis niloticus*) is the preferred species for culture worldwide due to their high rate of growth and tolerance to poor water quality conditions.

Blue tilapia (*Oreochromis aureus*) can tolerate lower water temperatures and are preferable in systems where low water temperature is an issue. Crossing a male blue tilapia with a female Nile tilapia creates a hybrid that has a high percentage of males (85-90%), grows fast to a large size, has good cold tolerance and tolerates a wide range of salinity.

[Male tilapia grow twice as fast as female tilapia. Therefore, having a high percentage of males or an all-male tilapia population is very desirable for the production of large uniform-sized fish. The standard procedure for obtaining all-male populations in the tilapia industry is the use of a male sex hormone (17-alpha methyltestosterone) to reverse the sex of tilapia. The hormone is administered through fish feed for the first 28 days of growth. During this period, fish that are genetically females will become males morphologically and grow as male fish although genetically they are still remain females.]

Mozambique tilapia (*Oreochromis mossambicus*) is very tolerant to high salinity and is the tilapia species cultured in California, which prohibits the introduction of other tilapia species.

There are many strains of red tilapia, but in general red tilapia have a lower growth rate and are less tolerant to poor water quality, but their growth rate and tolerance to poor water quality are still acceptable for commercial production. Both Mozambique and red tilapia can be grown in full strength seawater. The red color is a good marketing attribute if the fish are sold whole.

➤ Benefits of all male tilapia

Question

I've been reading a lot about the all-male tilapia populations and I understand that the males grow faster. Other than that, are there other benefits? If you have all male, do they get along or are there problems with them being territorial? Do you need a bigger tank for all male tilapia? Also, please tell me what kind of tilapia you raise, and why.

Answer

Male tilapia will grow at about twice the rate of female tilapia. Female tilapia devote a large portion of their energy to egg production rather than growth. If you use a mixed-sex population and the male tilapia reach a marketable weight of 1.5 lbs (680 g), the female tilapia will average about half that weight (0.75 lbs/340 g), which is not a marketable size. If you could find another market for smaller fish, time and effort would be required to sort (grade) the fish into two size groups. Additional labor is required, and the smaller fish would sell for a lower price. The goal in aquaculture is to produce uniform-sized fish at a desired weight on a fixed schedule, which can be accomplished with all-male populations.

Male tilapia are very territorial at low densities and constantly fight and even kill each other to defend their territory in small confined spaces such as a fish tank. However, at the high stocking densities used in aquaponic systems their territorial instinct breaks down and the fish develop a harmonious schooling behavior. In the UVI system the minimum stocking density is 77 fish/m^3, which produces a Nile tilapia with an average weight of 1.8 lbs (816 g) at harvest after 24 weeks of growth. The size of the tank does not matter. What is important is the density.

Nile tilapia (*Oreochromis niloticus*) is the most widely cultured species of tilapia in the world because of its rapid growth rate and hardiness. It has an attractive appearance, a good body conformation and is easy to breed.

➤ Process for converting to all male population

Question
Can you explain the different methods of getting an all male population of tilapia. I have heard about using hormones, but what is the process? What about genetic modification? Can you just sort them out rather than use either of these methods? I am interested in learning the pros and cons of each option.

Answer
The question you ask has been a major concern of the worldwide tilapia culture industry, which now produces more than 5 billion lbs of tilapia annually. The reason is that male tilapia

grow twice as fast as female tilapia. A tilapia producer wants to harvest large uniform-sized fish. And in pond culture, if there are females, there will be excessive reproduction, which leads to competition for food and stunting of the entire population. Aquaculturists are still conducting research on this problem. A book could be written to answer your question, so I must summarize and simplify my answer.

The industry standard for creating all-male populations is sex reversal. When a tilapia egg hatches and the fry absorbs its yolk sac, it is not sexually differentiated for a while although its sex is genetically predetermined. During this period fry are given feed that contains a male sex hormone (17-alpha methyltestosterone or MT) for 21 to 28 days. This hormone is a synthetic version of the testosterone found in male tilapia. However, during this short period, genetic females will become phenotypic (visible characteristic) males and grow as fast as males for the duration of their life cycle. When the hormone is withdrawn, the fry will weigh less than 0.5 g. It will then grow to 1.3 lb – 1.5 lb (600 - 700 g) over a 10-month period. MT breaks down and is no longer present. However, the Food and Drug Administration has studied the efficacy, food safety and environmental effects of MT for nearly 20 years through a program called Investigations in New Animal Drugs (INAD). The use of MT for tilapia sex reversal should soon acquire unqualified approval. In the meantime, tilapia hatcheries in the U.S. most pay a fee, register in the INAD Program and follow strict protocols.

Another method for obtaining all-male fingerlings is referred to as YY Supermales or Genetically Male Tilapia (GMT). In this method, tilapia breeding stocks are manipulated with hormones to produce a male tilapia that has YY chromosomes. A normal male has XY chromosomes while a female tilapia has XX chromosomes. Therefore when a supermale tilapia is bred with a female tilapia, all the progeny will be XY males. No hormones are administered to the fish that are raised for consumption. However, it is a difficult process to produce YY males. A breeder does not know which male fish is YY male. Therefore individual males are subjected to progeny testing. If all of the offspring develop as males, it can be safely assumed that it is an YY male. Needless to say, YY male brood stock is very expensive.

There are about 70 species of tilapia but only eight species have commercial significance. Crosses between some of these species can produce all-male hybrids. The most significant of these crosses is between a female Nile tilapia (*Oreochromis niloticus*) and a male Blue tilapia (*O. aureus*). The male hybrids from this cross express hybrid vigor. They grow faster and are stronger than either parent. This cross is popular in Israel and China. The drawback of relying on species crosses to produce all-male progeny is the difficulty of keeping the stocks separate and pure. This is especially difficult for the Nile X Blue tilapia cross because these species appear almost identical. This task can only be accomplished by major hatcheries with large and secure facilities and expert fish handlers. When species purity is lost, female fish will begin to materialize in the progeny.

Finally, the least technical but most inefficient method of obtaining male fingerlings is called "Hand Sexing." In this method fingerlings are reared to 4 inches in length 0.7-0.9 oz (20-25 g) and manually separated into groups of males and females. What distinguishes a female tilapia from a male tilapia is the presence of an oviduct on the genital papilla of the fish. The oviduct is absent in male tilapia. The oviduct appears as a groove oriented perpendicular to the axis of the body. The oviduct is difficult to see and can be highlighted by swabbing it with a dye such as crystal violet. This method is very laborious and inaccurate. A worker can separate about 2,000 fingerlings a day with an error rate of 10 to 20%. It is also a wasteful method because female fingerlings, which require feed, space and time to raise, must be discarded.

➢ Raising tilapia

Question

I am considering setting up a commercial aquaponics system in Virginia. I have looked around and see there are several tilapia suppliers in the US. The cost of the fingerlings plus the shipping is fairly high so I would rather raise my own if it is not too difficult. Can you tell me what is required and how difficult it is to raise the tilapia? What equipment do I need? Also, what is the process for raising all males?

Nile tilapia (Oreochromis niloticus) in a Clear Flow Aquaponic System® at Nelson and Pade, Inc.'s demonstration greenhouse, Montello, WI

Answer

You can breed tilapia and raise your own fingerlings, but there will be additional capital and operational expenses. Logistics will be complicated to ensure that the required number of sex-reversed fingerlings is ready on schedule. There will be increased demands on your time and management skills. I recommend that you initially start buying sex-reversed male fingerlings. If you are successful in growing and marketing tilapia, then Phase 2 of your operation could be expansion into breeding and sex-reversal.

Most hatcheries are located in the southern states to take advantage of a long breeding season under natural conditions. If you breed tilapia in the cooler north, you will have to control temperature and light (during winter) to simulate summer conditions. There are many types of breeding systems, but at the University of the Virgin Islands (UVI) we recommend a system that was developed at the Asian Institute of Technology (AIT) in Thailand. Although this system is used outdoor in ponds in Thailand, we have modified it to outdoor tanks. You could use it in indoor tanks. The breeding occurs in hapas, fine meshed nets that are suspended in the tanks and occupy nearly the entire volume of the tank. Small brood fish, weighing about 3.5 oz (100 g), are placed in the hapas at a density of 0.6 fish/ft^2 and a sex ratio of two females to one male. After 5 days, all of the breeding fish are collected for the removal of eggs from the female's mouth, where they are being incubated. Only a small portion of females will be carrying eggs on a given collection date. To catch the breeders, a floating pipe (bamboo in the case of Thailand) is pushed down the length of the hapa to concentrate all the brood fish in one area. Fish are caught one at a time with two scoop nets. The top net has large mesh and the lower net has fine mesh. If the female spits out the eggs, they will be captured in the lower net and not crushed by the female. Some females hold onto their eggs. Their mouth has to be opened with the collector's fingers for removal of eggs by dipping the female into the water repeatedly with the nets positioned underneath its mouth. The eggs are transferred to a hatching jar to complete incubation.

At this stage we have modified the AIT system. Water from a hatching jar flows into a hapa suspended in a tank. As the eggs hatch and the fry absorb their yolk sac, they will swim near the surface and be carried into the hapa. Their number is estimated and they are fed powered feed three times a day for 28 days. The feed contains 17-alpha methyltestosterone at a concentration of 60mg/kg. An initial feeding rate of 20% of body weight per day is gradually decreased based on a formula. At the end of this process, the fish weigh approximately 0.5 g and hopefully 100% of them are males although the system is not foolproof and there may be a few females. Actually all are phenotypically males (i.e., their external appearance is that of a male) although half are still genetically females. The reason for producing sex-reversed males is that males grow twice as fast as females. In a commercial fish culture operation, the goal is to have uniform sized fish at harvest. No additional hormones are administered after the first 28 days. The sex-reversal process has been studied extensively for nearly 20 years for efficacy, food safety and environmental impact and will be given final approval by FDA next year, although provisional approval has been in effect for a long time.

Once you have sex-reversed male tilapia, you will have to set up a nursery system to grow the fingerlings to an advanced size before they can be stocked into the growout system, the system where they will be cultured to marketable size. You would have to do this whether you buy sex-reversed fingerlings or produce your own. The UVI nursery system grows sex-reversed male fingerlings in a recirculating system to a size 1.8 oz (50 g) in 12 weeks at a stocking rate of 1000 fish/m^3.

I suggest you take our next short course where you will be taught the technique for producing sex-reversed fingerlings in much more detail and get hands-on experience.

Other Fish Species

> **Catfish**

Question

I can't get tilapia where I live (central California) but I have access to catfish fingerlings. Do you see any problem putting catfish in an aquaponic system? They mostly swim on the bottom. Will this cause any issues like stirring up the waste in the tank? Should I stock them at the same density as I would for tilapia? If you don't think catfish are a good choice, do you have other recommendations?

Answer

You could conduct a trial with catfish fingerlings. Try to obtain assurances that they are healthy. Catfish have been raised in aquaponic systems experimentally, but the culture of channel catfish at the commercial level in aquaponic systems has not caught on. One reason is that tilapia is more valuable than catfish. The farm bank price of catfish has not increased appreciably in the last 30 years, but operating costs have, and catfish farmers operate at very thin profit margins even in the best of times. Unfortunately, these are not the best of times. The recession, competition from imports, and a large increase in feed costs, due to the rising cost of corn and soybeans, is devastating the catfish industry, and production has decreased about 40% in the last couple years. Many Mississippi catfish farmers have drained their ponds and are now raising corn and soybeans in the nutrient-rich soils at the bottom of their large ponds which can exceed 20 acres (8 hectares) in size.

Another reason that catfish aquaponics or catfish culture in recirculating systems is uncommon is that catfish, as hardy as they look, are susceptible to a wide range of diseases. They do not do well at the high densities that tilapia can handle. Usually the availability of catfish fingerlings is also a problem because catfish breed once a year in the spring while tilapia breed throughout the year under warm water conditions, and tilapia fingerlings are always available from hatcheries in the southern states.

Tilapia may be better than catfish at stirring up the solid waste from the bottom of the tank. This is a good trait because the solids are then swept out of the rearing tank in the water current. Fish that swim in the middle of water column do not stir up solids, which will then accumulate on the bottom of the tank. As this solid organic waste decays, it produces ammonia and consumes oxygen.

A good option to tilapia is rainbow trout. They do well at densities as high as tilapia if good water quality is maintained. They require lower water temperatures, lower levels of ammonia and nitrite and higher levels of dissolved oxygen (DO). Maintaining water temperature at 70°F (21.1°C)is the high end of the range for rainbow trout. DO concentrations should always stay above 5 ppm (mg/liter), but fortunately colder water holds more oxygen. An additional biofiltration stage should be added to keep ammonia-nitrogen and nitrite-nitrogen levels below 1.0 ppm (mg/liter).

Other species that can be cultured in aquaponic systems in California include largemouth bass, yellow perch, bluegills and koi carp. Each of these species generally requires better water quality than tilapia. I recently learned of a move to eliminate the restrictions on raising tilapia in the central and northern areas of California. I hope this initiative is successful.

➢ Catfish vs. tilapia

Question

How long to do you think catfish would take to grow from fry to 1.5-2.0 lbs (680-907 g) in your average well- maintained aquaponic setup? Also, do you know the average fish density for catfish as compared to, say, tilapia in aquaponics? I'm only looking for a general guideline at the moment before I build my own system and test it for real. So, for illustration purposes, let's say it's a 10,000 gal (37.9 m³) tank. How many catfish should I put in there to keep mortality rates low and growth rates high. How long will it take the fish to reach 1.5 to 2.0 lbs (680-907 g) assuming near optimal feed rates? Also, if you have any good links that you could share please let me know.

Answer

Catfish fingerlings at 1.2 oz (35 g), stocked into a pond at 5,434 fish per acre can reach 1 lb (454 g) in 170 days (5.6 months). That's a growth rate of 2.5 g/day. If they continued to grow at that rate they would reach 1.5 lbs in 258 days (8.5 months) and 2.0 lbs in 349 days (11.5 months). However, they would probably grow faster than 2.5 g/day as they became larger. In ponds, growth slows dramatically during winter but an aquaponic system can maintain optimum water temperatures for year-round growth.

On the other hand, catfish have never performed well in recirculating systems due to disease problems. Plus, the economics are not favorable for raising catfish in recirculating systems. In March of this year the price farmers were receiving for whole catfish was $0.56/lb, which is very low. There is a controversy ranging over the importation of basa catfish from Vietnam. These are not a channel catfish but they taste the same to most consumers and the Vietnamese are very good at producing these low cost fish. You will need to develop a niche market for your catfish to obtain a better price. You may have to process and sell direct to restaurants. If you have a 10,000 gal (37.9 m^3) tank as part of a recirculating system that purifies the water effectively and maintains adequate dissolved oxygen levels, you should aim for a final density of 0.5 lbs/gal (60 kg/m^3). This is a conservative density. If you want 1.5 lb (680 g) fish, you would stock 3,300 fish per tank. If you want 2 lb (907 g) fish, you would stock 2,500 fish per tank.

> ## Barramundi

Question

I am interested in making a closed circuit aquaponic farm in either Delaware or Maryland. Instead of growing tilapia, I would like to grow barramundi. Have you worked with this fish? Is the equipment for raising tilapia in aquaponics suitable for Barramundi? I am looking to grow 150,000 lbs (68,039 kg) of barramundi per year, plus whatever vegetables you recommend to service restaurants in East Coast cities with live, whole fish.

Answer

Barramundi (*Lates calcarifer*), also known as Asian seabass, is a hardy fish that grows quickly at high densities in recirculating or aquaponic systems. Barramundi are commonly cultured in Australia in recirculating systems. A previous article in Aquaponic Journal (issue #47, 4th quarter, 2007) by Malcolm Taylor describes his success in growing leafy green vegetables and barramundi in an aquaponic system using raft culture.

Currently the best approach for a commercial barramundi operation in the U.S. is to obtain fertilized eggs or sac fry (hatched fry that are still living off their egg yolk) from Australia where there are commercial hatcheries. Culturing the larvae to a fingerling size is challenging. The barramundi larvae are fed zooplankton (rotifers) initially followed by brine shrimp (*Artemia*) larvae (nauplii). Algal culture is required to raise rotifers. The larvae must eventually be weaned off live food onto a formulated high protein diet. During this period the larvae are very predacious and must be graded frequently to separate them into groups of fish that similar in size. Even then it is not uncommon for two fish of the same size to try to eat each other. One fish gets stuck in the other's mouth and they both die.

I recommend that barramundi culture be staggered to provide a constant supply of fish to the market. However, since the logistics of shipping seed stock from Australia is difficult and fingerling rearing is complicated, shipments should be limited to three or four per year. Not all of the fingerlings would be stocked into the rearing tanks at the same time. Some would have to be held in a nursery and stocked into the rearing tanks at predetermined intervals.

Barramundi is euryhaline, which means it can grow in full strength seawater as well as freshwater. There is some anecdotal evidence that marine fish are intolerant to high potassium levels, but this has not been verified through research nor have potentially toxic levels been determined. An operator should be aware of this issue and try to maintain potassium at a minimum level for good plant growth.

➢ Koi

Question

Has anyone tried using Koi in an aquaponic system? They are supposedly very hardy, and fairly temperature and water quality tolerant. Even though there would be no "food" value, they seem to have a market to collectors/enthusiasts.

Answer

Rebecca Nelson and John Pade, Nelson and Pade, Inc., have used koi carp in their aquaponic system with good success. Aquaponic systems are ideal for raising koi carp on a commercial basis, if you follow the guidelines for fish in general in regards to stocking rates (harvest density, 0.5 lbs/gal) and water quality. This is a much higher density than that used to stock decorative ponds where koi carp are displayed. I say "ideal" because koi carp grow well at water temperatures that plants prefer (70-75°F/21.1-23.9°C) unlike tilapia, which do best at higher temperatures (80-85°F/26.7-29.4°C).

Koi carp are an ornamental strain of the common carp (*Cyprinus carpio*) and are very hardy. However, when you receive new fingerlings or brood stock, you should quarantine them for several weeks in a designated recirculating system or pond. You do not want to introduce any parasites or diseases into your aquaponic system because you cannot treat them in a system with edible plants. Being an ornamental fish, there are more treatment options to combat disease for koi carp, but the plants may absorb the therapeutic chemicals.

After the new fish get a clean bill of health, there should no problems. When you have a good strain of koi carp, work out a breeding system and minimize new introductions. A single koi carp with an excellent color pattern can sell for tens of thousands of dollars. Even standard koi carp retail for $12.00 to $25.00 each depending on size. Aquaponics enhances the profit potential of koi carp production by providing excellent water quality, a stable environment and valuable byproducts such as vegetables, culinary herbs or flowers.

➢ Freshwater shrimp

Question

I am in the process of doing research and planning for a new indoor shrimp / prawn / crawfish farm in Montana. I am trying to find out if you have had any experience in cultivating fresh water shrimp in one of your aquaponic systems? Any information you could provide would be greatly appreciated.

Answer

It seems like you are biting off more than you can chew if you want to grow shrimp, prawns and crawfish in an indoor facility. All of these species have specific culture requirements that are not interchangeable. Moreover, freshwater prawns and crawfish require low stocking densities due to their territorial and cannibalistic nature. I believe that high density indoor culture of freshwater prawns or crawfish would not be technically or economically feasible. Low salinity shrimp culture may have potential as densities as high as 5 kg/m^3 have been obtained in recirculating systems. It will be a challenge to achieve an ionic composition that is suitable for both shrimp and hydroponic plants.

Low salinity shrimp culture is practiced with Pacific white shrimp (*Litopenaeus vannamei*). A minimum salinity of 2 ppt (two parts per thousand) can be used. This is equivalent to 2,000 ppm (parts per million), which is the initial nutrient concentration of most hydroponic solutions. However, sodium and chloride ions are kept to a minimum in hydroponic solutions (< 50 ppm) while shrimp require substantially higher concentrations of sodium and chloride ions for osmoregulation. Shrimp also benefit if the levels of potassium, magnesium, manganese and sulfate ions are increased. Adding these ions, which are plant nutrients, should benefit hydroponic plants. The vegetables used in a shrimp aquaponic system must be tolerant to high concentrations of sodium and chloride. For example, tomatoes tolerate high concentrations of sodium chloride.

Under intensive culture, stocking densities of 250 shrimp/m^3 are common. Let me be very speculative here because I have thought about the potential of raising shrimp in the UVI commercial aquaponic system. We have four rearing tanks that are each 2,060 gal (7.8 m^3). Assume that we stock each tank at a rate of 250 shrimp/m^3, culture them for 16 weeks to a size of 0.7 oz (20 g), and stagger the production as we do with tilapia. Also assume that survival is 90%. There would be 13 harvests a year. Each harvest would be 77.3 lbs (7.8 x 250 x 0.90 x 20 divided by 454 g/lb). Total annual production would be 1,005 lbs (455 kg). Current annual production of tilapia in this system is 11,000 lbs (4,990 kg), but we sell them for $2.50/lb, while live shrimp could probably be sold for $8.00/lb or more in certain markets. Since production is roughly 10% of our current tilapia production, the plant growing area could be reduced by 90%, which means that the ratio of surface areas devoted to plants and shrimp would be approximately 1:1, respectively (it is now 11.5:1), so more space can be devoted to building shrimp rearing tanks. There are many assumptions here and many areas that need to be researched.

> ## Poly-culture of fish and crustaceans

Question

Has anyone demonstrated success in combining such species

as tilapia and crawfish in the fish tank in aquaponics? Are there problems associated with introducing several species of fish with similar temperature and water quality needs? I'd like to make my system as diverse as I can, especially among life forms which are mutually beneficial to each other.

Answer

A limited number of crawfish could be raised with tilapia but I would not attempt it. Crawfish need space to prevent cannibalism and, therefore, the stocking rate would have to be very low. You do not want crawfish to enter the hydroponic beds if you are using raft culture because they will eat plant roots. Crawfish prefer a habitat that provides hiding places. However, aquaponic rearing tanks need an unobstructed bottom so that solid waste can be easily removed. You could use a few crawfish for show but they would not be an important component of the system.

As for fish polyculture, there are many possibilities. Rebecca Nelson and John Pade of Nelson and Pade, Inc., publisher of the Aquaponics Journal have raised largemouth bass, koi carp and black crappie and catfish together. There are some limitations. You cannot raise a coldwater trout with a warm-water catfish or a highly predacious species with its prey, but most fish will live harmoniously together if acceptable water quality is maintained. Aquarium fish offer a good example. Many species can be raised together.

I doubt that you would find mutually beneficial species for a rearing tank. Polyculture is generally practiced in fertilized or manured ponds where there are many feeding niches. Each species will feed on a different type of food organism, thereby increasing total production of the pond. Fish in aquaponic systems are generally given a formulated feed and there are no natural organisms of significance to supplement their diet. A problem with polyculture is sorting the species at harvest, as each species usually needs to be marketed separately.

Food Safety

> ## Fish Processing

Question

I plan on selling some fish soon and might have to gut the fish to get a better price. Does that require me to get licensed from the FDA or another governmental agency? What is involved in the certification and process? I would like to sell directly to the restaurants and not sure if they will take whole fish. Thanks!

Answer

If restaurants are willing to accept a whole fish, by all means aim for that market. However, Americans abhor bones in their fish and usually prefer fillets, which for tilapia dress out at 33% of the whole fish. The economic returns for fillets are not as good as that of whole fish. You might want to search for the whole fish market in your area before you resort to processing.

If you do process, you have to develop a HACCP Plan (Hazard Analysis and Critical Control Points). HACCP information can be found on a web site at the University of California, Davis (http://seafood.ucdavis.edu/). You will also need to follow a list of federal regulations known as Sanitary Standard Operating Procedures (SSOP), which can be found at the following web site: http://www.access.gpo.gov/nara/cfr/waisidx_03/21cfr110_03.html You may need a license from your local health department or your state department of agriculture. Contact a county agent at the Cooperative Extension Service for information on local requirements. You will not need a license from the Food and Drug Administration, but FDA will inspect your facility to ensure that you are complying with your HACCP Plan. Good luck.

➤ E-coli and coliforms

Question

What steps are taken in aquaponics to ensure that bacteria associated with fish solid waste do not contaminate crops to be consumed by humans?

Answer

Pathogenic organisms that enter water through fecal contamination are very difficult to isolate and identify. However, coliform bacteria, which are present in large quantities in the intestinal tracts of humans and warm-blooded animals are easily tested and commonly used to indicate fecal contamination. Each person discharges from 100 to 400 billion coliform bacteria per day. They aid digestion through the breakdown of food. The presence of coliforms does not always mean contamination with human or animal waste as some species can grow in soil but *Escherichia* coli (*E. coli*) are entirely of fecal origin. Drinking water is considered safe when less than 5% of water samples test positive for total coliform bacteria. However, those samples testing positive must be tested for fecal coliforms. No fecal coliforms are allowed in drinking water but the standard for recreational water is 235 organisms/100 ml in a single sample. There are hundreds of strains of *E. coli* that are harmless. However, one strain, identified as O157:H7 and associated with cattle feces, creates powerful toxins and has caused many illnesses and deaths.

Aquaponic systems could be exposed to fecal contamination from warm-blooded animals. In an outdoor system contamination could come from birds for example.

In an indoor system contamination could come from rodents. However, the dose would be quite small and it would not occur regularly. Any coliform bacteria that get into the system would be highly diluted. I doubt that there would be any contamination from cattle feces. In the 20 years we have been growing plants aquaponically at the University of the Virgin Islands, no one has ever gotten ill. In the past we raised mainly lettuce, which was washed but not cooked to kill bacteria. Normally the leaves do not contact with the culture water, but some water gets on the leaves from splashing or during packaging operations. Look at the alternative, which is field production of lettuce. Manures are often used as a soil amendment, including cattle manure. During rainstorms, soil splashes on the leaves. A field is a more natural habitat for birds, mice, rats, rabbits, squirrels, etc. The issue should be studied. In the meantime, I would not be overly concerned about microbial health risks in aquaponic systems.

Question

We are newly getting into building our Aquaponic system and am having problems with passing the Food and Safety test for our fish water with E. coli showing up in the test. What would be the best solution to correct the problem?

Answer

You probably do not have a water quality problem as much as you have a water quality regulator problem. Coliforms are naturally present in the environment; as well as feces while fecal coliforms and *E. coli*, which is short for *Escherichia coli,* only come from human and animal fecal waste. They are not a health threat in themselves but are used to indicate whether other potentially harmful bacteria may be present. The human digestive tract contains billions of *E. coli*. Although most strains of *E. coli* are harmless, others can make you sick. The worst strain (*E. coli* O157:H7) is deadly and usually elicits nationwide headlines and recalls of fresh fruit and vegetables.

I am going to quote heavily from an article on the Internet (http://groups.ucanr.org/UC_GAPs/Elimanate_Fecal_Coliforms/) that was published by the University of California, Agriculture and Natural Resources. The article is listed under the category: University of California Good Agriculture Practices (GAP). It is subtitled "Eliminate Fecal Coliforms from Your Vegetable and Fruit Safety Vocabulary."

The article states that "developing fruit and vegetable microbial standards, food safety management and certification plans, or setting regional water policy, basing decisions on total numbers of 'Coliform' bacteria or 'Fecal Coliforms' is not supported by current science." Fecal Coliforms are a group of organisms that can be practically measured in a laboratory and they may "indicate" or be associated with harmful pathogens.

"The problem is that this association just does not seem to hold up when evaluating irrigation water, run-off water, or typical product safety. To be a useful indicator of hygienic standards and water management decisions, the following assumptions must be true for 'Fecal Coliforms' in each setting where samples are collected and analyzed: 1) The only source of these bacteria is feces, manure, septic run-off, or sewage 2) There is no significant source in the environment unrelated to these primary sources 3) The indicator bacteria do not multiply in soil, water, and especially do not multiply significantly on the surface of crops, surrounding vegetation or rangeland plants."

"Research over many years has shown that the current, general grouping called 'Fecal Coliforms' most often fails in each of these assumptions when talking about horticultural commodities and water under the influence of run-off from production locations. The predominant numbers of bacteria that test positive in assays for 'Fecal Coliform' from horticultural production and postharvest handling operations are benign or non-pathogenic soil and leaf colonizers."

"What are the consequences? 1) Uninformed individuals see high numbers of "fecal" bacteria from produce or water samples and assume the grower's fruit or vegetable is not marketable 2) Some GAP and food safety planners and auditors erect impractical and unnecessary standards for microbial content 3) Some service providers use the data to sell unnecessary and potentially ineffective sanitation systems that provide no assurance of freedom from true pathogen contamination 4) Ag-water use and management policies may be developed without the benefit of a sound risk assessment."

"What indicator is best? *E. coli* has been suggested as the preferred indicator of fecal contamination in fresh water sources and on produce. The Environmental Protection Agency (EPA) cites *E. coli* as the best indicator of microbial water quality in recreational freshwater systems. The EPA levels are not strictly applicable to developing irrigation water standards but serve as useful guidance for current research and practical approaches to on-farm food safety system development.

Non-pathogenic *E. coli* have most of the traits of a "Recommended Indicator" (listed above) and the cost of monitoring is not prohibitive for most growers and shippers. Unfortunately, several years of research has shown that the predictive correlation between *E. coli* and the presence of human pathogens, including viruses and parasites, is highly inconsistent or entirely lacking in many applications for fruit and vegetable production and postharvest handling. In addition, recent reports have found that *E. coli* has the ability to multiply in tropical production environments, thereby mistakenly elevating the apparent risk and concern. However, it is the best we have for now. Monitoring for pathogens is impractical and too costly while other promising indicators, such as viruses of *E. coli*, persist much longer in the environment than many pathogens. Finding better indicators is an active area of research at many institutions."

The article includes this diagram to indicate the relationships between various coliform bacteria and pathogens. Pathogens form So what can you do to obtain approval? Two websites with

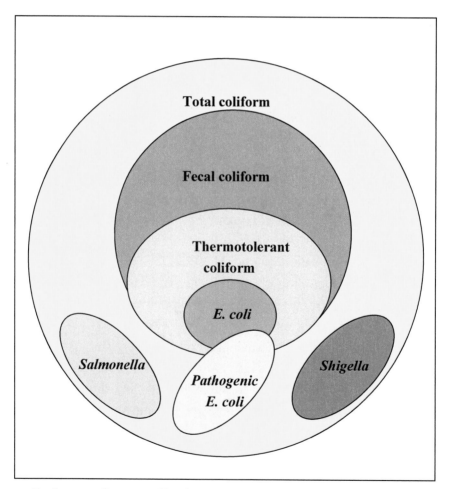

Pathogens form small subgroups of the total coliform picture.

"additional background information, resource contacts, and links to GAP development and on-farm self-audit resources" are listed in the article (http://ucgaps.ucdavis.edu and http://vric.ucdavis.edu).

You can use these to establish "Good Agricultural Practices" for your aquaponic system and possibly find the *E. coli* source. The key is to disinfect your source water and keep animals away from your facility. This should be relatively easy if the aquaponic system is in a greenhouse. If it is outside, I suggest covering it with netting to keep birds out and erect a barrier near the ground to prevent the entry of rodents. You will probably discover other entry points for *E. coli* and prevention techniques as you do the on-farm self-audit. Good luck.

➢ Shrimp farming in China

Question

I have 2 questions. First, the grocery stores have been offering inexpensive shrimp & prawns lately. I bought a bag that said, "fish farmed, Dalian, China". Do you know if the farming methods are sanitary and sustainable? My second question is based on the article in Vol. VI, No. 4, "Build a hobby system." I plan on setting up an aquaponic system on my screened patio. It is hot: 80 – 100⁰ F (26.6-37.8⁰C) 6 months/year and cold the other. I only want to use the system in the hot season. Can you suggest a fish type for perhaps a 50 gal (1.9 m³) tank?

Answer

There are many environmental, social and food safety issues surrounding shrimp culture. Some of the environmental issues include loss of mangroves or agricultural land for pond construction, intrusion of saline water, pollution of coastal water and loss of biodiversity. The environmental impact of shrimp culture has heightened concern among a wide spectrum of global organizations (governments, environmental groups, researchers, industry associations) and has led to the development of a Code of Conduct for Responsible Fisheries, including shrimp aquaculture, by the Food and Agricultural Organization of the United Nations. The Code establishes voluntary codes of practice (e.g., disease control, use of drugs and chemicals, monitoring impacts of shrimp culture, sound engineering practices) for sustainable shrimp culture. The Code helps countries establish a legal framework to authorize and regulate shrimp farms. Since shrimp aquaculture accounts for nearly one third of world shrimp output and employs hundreds of thousands of people, it is essential to implement the Code to ensure sustainable production. This is the goal, but populous, developing countries like China cannot always meet the goal as it produces nearly 200 million pounds of shrimp annually on more than 6,000 farms.

A particularly troublesome problem occurred early last year when residues of the antibiotic cloramphenicol were found in imported shrimp from China and other Asian countries, leading to a ban on imports from China in Europe and increased inspections of Chinese seafood in the U.S. In human medicine, chloramphenicol is considered a drug of last resort because excessive exposure can cause potentially fatal aplastic anemia in one of every 30,000 people treated. The detection of chloramphenicol has led to the impoundment and destruction of seafood shipments from several Asian countries, resulting in the loss of millions of dollars. Seafood importers must now verify that no residues are present in their shipments. Verifications are backed up with FDA inspections of overseas operations and testing of imports. Asian counties have also mounted large efforts to rectify this problem, which jeopardizes their shrimp export industries.

Sanitary conditions are not generally a problem. Processing plants in China that export to the U.S. are inspected and approved by USDA.

In summary, there is a chance that the shrimp you buy from China may not be produced in an environmentally sustainable manner or may have antibiotic residues. The probability is small, and some of the profits from your purchase may go towards industry development and long-term resolution of these problems.

In response to your second question, if the aquaponic system is designed properly and stocked and fed within the capacity of its filtration system, a wide range of fish can be used. Tilapia is the most common fish used in aquaponic systems, but California has many restrictions on the culture of tilapia. You better check the legality of using tilapia with the state fisheries department. Other fish include hybrid stripped bass, largemouth bass, bluegills, carp, catfish, and ornamental fish. It would be too warm in the summer for trout, but they could be raised in the winter. I would select a fish species that is available at local hatcheries and grows well on pelletized feed.

Alternative Methods

➢ **Low-cost system using bamboo instead of PVC**

Question

I am a student from the Philippines and I am studying crop science. I would like to ask a question regarding aquaponics. For our school project/special problem class, we are to design our own hydroponic or aquaponic model using low cost and recycled materials. We decided to use bamboo instead of PVC pipe and feed the plants with an ebb and flow system. The bamboo will be hung horizontally and is arranged in such a way that excess water (with nutrients) from bamboo #1 (top) goes to bamboo #2 (middle) and then to bamboo #3 (bottom). I would like to know if the water with nutrient from bamboo # 1 can flow to bamboo # 2 and to # 3 without any problems. Do you see any disadvantage of this process?

Answer

Let me congratulate you on trying to develop low cost aquaponic systems for tropical countries. This is an area that needs more research to realize the potential of aquaponics. It seems that bamboo would be more appropriate for a nutrient film technique than an ebb and flow system. Ebb and flow systems are usually used with a growing media that supports the plant such as gravel.

During the ebb cycle, water is drained from the media to draw in air, which provides oxygen to the plant roots and bacteria. On the flow cycle, water floods the media and brings nutrients to the plant roots and metabolites (in the case of aquaponics) to the bacteria for treatment (removal).

In your situation a continuous flow of a thin layer of water would nourish the plants roots. Air above the water layer would provide oxygen to the roots. I think it would be better to arrange several bamboo shoots (tubes) in just one tier. Orient the tubes at a slight angle so that water will flow through them. Select the largest bamboo possible. Bamboo has internal partitions at each node. You will have to break out these partitions to create a continuous hallow tube. Cut circular holes in the top of the bamboo tubes to insert seedlings. Use two additional bamboo tubes, oriented perpendicular to the growing tubes, to deliver and collect the aquaculture effluent.

Bamboo may not provide enough surface area for sufficient biofiltration. Solid waste in the effluent could accumulate in the bamboo tubes, blocking water flow and creating unhealthy, anaerobic (no oxygen) conditions. Therefore, you should install a good solids removal device and a biofilter in the aquaponic system. The aquaculture effluent should flow through the solids removal component first and then the biofilter before it enters the bamboo hydroponic component. Good luck with the your system.

➢ Irrigating soil crops with aquaculture waste water

Question

We have a 1400 acre (567 hectares) ranch in Nebraska. Our nitrogen bill is approaching $50,000.00 per season. We are looking for economically positive solutions to this cost. We are researching sustainable alternatives to producing enough nitrogen to run our operation. We know we can set up a feedlot of cattle to produce manure rich in nutrients to replenish our soil (Loam). We *are also looking at the feasibility of setting up an aquaponics system which would feed into our irrigation system. We have 480 acres of irrigated land through a pivot system. These systems have chemigation units that allow us to disperse nutrients in liquid form as we irrigate. Before doing a feasibility study we need to know how large a fish farm would we have to have in order to generate 110 tons of 35% liquid nitrogen Do you have any idea?*

Answer

Nitrogen concentrations, as nitrate-nitrogen, will only reach about 500 ppm in aquaculture water before they cause problems for the fish if you are raising a hardy fish like tilapia for example. That concentration is only 0.05%, far short of 35%. This high concentration (500 ppm) would adversely affect hydroponic vegetable production. Therefore you would have to maintain even lower nitrate-nitrogen levels. The rest of the nitrogen would be in the form of solid waste. The total amount of nitrogen required to fertilize 480 acres of land would be 77,000 lbs (110 tons x 2,000 lbs/ton x 0.35 = 77,000 lbs). Tilapia utilize 32.5% of the nitrogen in fish feed for growth. Therefore, 67.5% of the nitrogen in fish feed becomes a waste product that could be used to fertilize field crops. Standard tilapia feed (32% protein) contains approximately 5% nitrogen. The amount of fish feed required to generate 77,0000 lbs of waste nitrogen would be 2,369,000 lbs [(0.675) (0.05) X = 77,0000 lbs] based on dry weight feed (feed containing moisture would weigh 11% more - 2,632,000 lbs) and the assumption that all of the waste nitrogen can be recovered, which is not realistic because a considerable amount of nitrogen is lost to the atmosphere as nitrogen gas through the process of denitrification. Therefore, much more feed would be required.

Assuming a feed conversion ratio of 1.5, which is equivalent to feed efficiency of 0.67 (1 ÷ 1.5 = 0.67), the use of 2,632,000 lbs of feed would produce 1,763,000 lbs of tilapia. Raising this much fish profitably would be a considerable challenge involving a huge capital outlay, many employees and an innovative marketing system to say the least, especially since you are in a cold climate and would need an environmentally-controlled indoor system. Raising grain would be an incidental activity compared to the amount of time and manpower you would have to devote to raising fish and vegetables. Also most of the nitrogen would be in a solid organic form. Therefore you would have to use a manure spreader to apply it rather than an irrigation system. The sludge would be generated continuously but would only be incorporated into the soil prior to planting. Hence a large aerated (to reduce denitrification) sludge storage pond would be required. My advice is to continue buying nitrogen, which I know is getting expensive, or try the cattle feed lot route.

➤ Pond aquaponics

Question

I have a backyard pond (approx. 1000 gal (3.8 m³), in full sun, using a biofilter), with lots of Koi. It has been a successful pond for about seven years, with clear water and Koi reproducing every spring like crazy (too many, too big for this small pond). I am about to sell the Koi and replace them with smaller fish (not to eat).

Questions: would I be able to grow a few vegetables aquaponically in this pond? Would I need more techno-gadgets and filters than the biofilter I already have? Is there a kind of fish that would be compatible with growing vegetables? Is the sun a problem?

Answer

If the pond is in full sunlight and the water is clear, then the nutrient levels must be low or there would be an algal bloom. Perhaps a portion of the pond is shaded by aquatic plants that are removing nutrients or there is a high water exchange rate, which could account for low nutrient levels. Or maybe the stocking and feeding rates are too low to allow much nutrient accumulation.

In any event, there will not be enough nutrients to raise vegetables if there are not enough nutrients to create an algal bloom, as indicated by green colored water. Also vegetables cannot be raised directly in the pond because the koi will eat the roots. Predator fish such as bass or perch will not affect plant roots.

In aquaponic systems the fish and the plants are raised in separate tanks, and all tank surfaces are shaded from the sun to avoid the growth of algae. The final harvest density in the fish rearing tank is generally 0.5 lbs/gal. This means the 1,000 gal (3.8 m^3) pond would produce 500 lbs (227 kg) of fish per crop. Raising this much fish will require some additional tanks to remove the solid waste. If you are interested in aquaponics, I suggest building a new system from scratch and continue to enjoy your koi or whatever fish you decide to raise.

➤ Sand culture with pond effluent

Question

I am a student in Thailand. I have been monitoring catfish pond water and after 14 weeks the water quality is as follows: NH4 3.14 mg/l, NO$_2$ 0.02 mg/l, NO$_3$ 0.17mg/l, TKN 11.3 mg/l, SRP 0.028 mg/l and TP 0.89 mg/l. The water temperature is 31°C, pH 7.21 and DO less than 1 mg/l. The pond is stocked with 6,000 catfish (200 m^2) and fed with pellet feed at 5 percent daily. Based *on this information, can you answer my questions below?*

➤ *Are there sufficient nutrients to grow lettuce in sand culture?
If so, how should I design the water flow rates from the pond to
lettuce?*

➤ *What should the retention time of the pond water in the sand
culture for the lettuce be?*

➤ *What filtration system should I use?*

Answer

I do not think your system will be feasible for growing lettuce.
Your nutrient levels are very low compared to the levels found in
aquaponic systems. For example, in a recent okra production trial,
the average nitrate-nitrogen concentration was 26.3 ppm (mg/liter)
(compared to your nitrate level of 0.17 mg/liter) and the average
orthophosphate concentration was 15.0 mg/liter (compared to your
soluble reactive phosphorus level of 0.028 mg/liter). Our fish
stocking density varies from 77-154 fish/m^3 (compared to your
stocking density of 3 fish/m^3, assuming your pond is 3 ft (1 m)
deep. Also your water temperature is a little too high at 87.8°F
(31°C). Our highest summertime water temperature reaches 84°F
(29°C) and the lettuce struggles a little at this temperature. We
shade the water surface to maintain lower water temperatures. We
maintain much higher levels of dissolved oxygen (5-7 mg/liter)
than the concentrations (less than 1 mg/liter) in your pond. There
are 11 other nutrients to consider, many of which would probably
be deficient in the pond water.

Another problem you will run into with sand is that it will
quickly clog and probably become anaerobic, which will kill the
lettuce roots. I know that Thai catfish ponds have very high
concentrations of suspended solids. These solids will be filtered
out by the sand, which will cause the sand to clog and block the
flow of water.

Maybe you should divert the pond water through aerated

channels using raft culture. However, I would not be overly optimistic that this will work because of the low nutrient levels and because suspended solids will adhere to the roots, blocking the uptake of water and nutrients. I suggest you remove the suspended solids before they enter the channels and I suggest setting up a two-stage solids removal system using two separate tanks. The first stage would use a settling tank with a 20-minute retention time to removal settleable solids. The second stage would use orchard netting to filter out the fine solids. These tanks would have to be cleaned periodically.

In the United States an experiment, which was conducted 1975, determined that the use of channel catfish pond water was not feasible for growing plants hydroponically. The nutrient levels were simply too low. In closed recirculating systems nutrients accumulate and nutrient concentrations approach the levels found in hydroponic nutrient solutions.

> ## Green water aquaculture

Question
I have a few questions about the Green Water tank process you are using at the University of the Virgin Islands for raising Tilapia.

>   *What does this water clarifier look like? Do you have any plans or sketches on the Internet?*

>   *At what rate do you turn the water over? Does all this water go through the clarifier or do you utilize a mechanical filter somehow?*

>   *Do the tilapia raised in this environment taste the same? Are they "muddy" in taste?*

I live in Arizona where warm temperatures are common almost all year so I am considering this for raising Tilapia. I have not seen any other work on this so it is very interesting to me that you have proven a system that works in the Virgin Islands.

Answer

We have just finished constructing a commercial-scale greenwater tank that is 52,000 gal (200 m³). The tank is made from core-filled concrete blocks with a 30-mil high-density polyethylene liner which covers the block walls and the earthen bottom. The tank bottom has a 3-degree slope from the side to the center where there is a 264 gal (1-m³) fiberglass cone with a 45-degree slope that leads to a 4 inch (10-cm) PVC drain line. We have eliminated the separate clarifier. We open an external knife-gate valve to remove sludge once a day. We have stocked this tank with 4,000 tilapia fingerlings and are currently feeding about 44 lbs (20 kg) of feed per day which produces about 52.9 gal (200 liters) of sludge. Since we are early in the production trial we are aerating with only one ¾-hp vertical lift pump. We are prepared to add two more pumps when they are needed. We have tilted a second ¾-hp vertical lift pump on its side to generate a circular flow in the tank to move solids toward the central clarifier. This pump is producing one rotation around the perimeter of the tank every 1.5 minutes. There is no turnover of water or mechanical filtration, just daily solids removal and weekly replacement of water lost by evaporation or solids removal. Biofiltration takes place in the water column by nitrifying bacteria attached to suspended organic particles. If this tank performs as well as our 30-m³ experimental units, it will produce 15,000 lbs (6,800 kg) of tilapia annually in two crops. We have not experienced off-flavors in tilapia cultured in our greenwater tank systems.

You can read a review of all our work on greenwater tank culture in a chapter (An Integrated Fish and Field Crop System for Arid Areas, pages 263-286) that I wrote for Ecological Aquaculture: The Evolution of the Blue Revolution, Barry A. Costa-Pierce, editor, 2002, Blackwell Science.

Research and Education

> ## ➤ History of aquaponics

Question

What is the history of Aquaponics?

Answer

Good question. I will give you my perspective on the history of modern aquaponics. There was an ancient system used in the Americas where a tightly matted bed of reeds was floated on lakes and used to grow plants. I assume, however, that the main purpose was irrigation with nutrients being applied as manures to the reed mats.

More recently, a man by the name of Leonard Pampel, working for the Milwaukee County Zoo in the late 1950s, developed an aquaponic system of sorts to purify water in the aviary building by using some terrestrial plant beds containing wheat and other plants to extract nutrients. The nutrients came mainly from dead fish and bird waste but the system worked spectacularly and he obtained a patent on it. I knew Mr. Pampel and he helped me set up aquariums using aquatic plants to extract waste nutrients and purify fish culture water. In the late 60s and early 70s there were a couple of attempts to use raceway effluent and fish pond water to grow terrestrial plants but they did not do well because the nutrient

223

levels were too low.

Then in the late 70s interest in aquaponics blossomed and several investigators, myself included, started using recirculating systems with minimal water exchange to accumulate waste nutrients to levels that approached those found in hydroponic systems. The first well documented paper was published in 1977 by Dr. William Lewis and others at the University of Southern Illinois in Carbondale. However, Dr. Lewis supplemented liberally with fertilizers and did quantify the full benefit of the fish effluent to terrestrial plants. Since then, many papers have been published and several M.S. and Ph.D. degrees were earned with aquaponics as the research topic. Back then we were calling these integrated systems.

The first time I saw the word "aquaponics" was in an article in the "Alternate Aquaculture Newsletter," published by Rodale Press. I don't know if the author coined this term or not, but it made perfect sense because up to that point an integrated system could have been anything. The term "aquaponics" defines the concept perfectly (aquaculture plus hydroponics) and now people know exactly what type of system is being referred to. Let me conclude by saying that the history of aquaponics has been short and its widespread application and greatest contributions lie in the future.

> **Continuing research in aquaponics**

Question
   Please tell me what specific areas of aquaponics you have been studying at the University of the Virgin Islands and also what areas you will study in the coming years. What research still

needs to be done in aquaponics? What other Universities are doing related research in recirculating aquaponic systems?

Answer

We have two aquaponic experiments planned for the immediate future. In our commercial-scale aquaponic system, we will be evaluating the production of watermelons, cantaloupe and honeydew melons. We want to determine production per plant growing area during one crop cycle. Based on the results of this experiment, we will select the most promising melon and evaluate three varieties and possibly two planting densities. A considerable amount of research is needed to obtain accurate estimates of annual production for dozens of plant crops in the UVI system, which uses polystyrene rafts. This information is needed to prepare enterprise budgets and business plans for commercial operations.

In our six replicated aquaponic systems, we are preparing a series of experiments to evaluate the production of chives, mint and watercress. We will not use rafts as these plants grow by spreading. Net pots, which support plants in rafts, restrict this type of growth. For mint and watercress we have lowered the water level to a depth of 6 inches and placed the plants on a shelf of vinyl covered wire mesh. The plants are growing well and spreading quickly over the entire surface of the hydroponic bed. Chives will be placed directly on the tank bottom, and the water depth will be lowered to 2 inches. We are trying to develop a mechanism for supporting the chives while they spread over the tank bottom. The goal of this project is to determine annual plant production levels, the best feeding rate ratio for plant production and the water treatment capacity of these plants. The underside of rafts (polystyrene sheets) provide considerable surface area for the growth of nitrifying bacteria, which improve water quality by removing ammonia and nitrite, which are toxic fish waste metabolites. By removing the rafts, the water treatment capacity of the hydroponic tanks will be reduced. In addition, there will be less water in the hydroponic tanks, which will lead to a faster turnover rate. We need to study the impacts of these changes on water quality and fish production.

Aquaponics is in its infancy as an industry and much more research has to be conducted in the future compared to what has been accomplished so far. Some general areas involve the evaluation of new fish species and fish/plant combinations, production levels of numerous high value plant crops, system designs and solid removal techniques, the effect of different feed formulations, including all plant protein fish feeds, on plant production and nutrient dynamics, the assessment of biological control methods for plant pests and diseases and the development of simple and inexpensive systems that can be used in developing counties. The systems that evolve from this research must be subjected to a rigorous economic assessment. Financers need assurance that aquaponic food production is profitable, sustainable and competitive with other production methods.

There are no universities that I know with an established a research program in aquaponics similar to that at UVI. Students from several universities have conducted research on aquaponics to obtain M.S. or Ph.D. degrees, but these are isolated studies that reflected a student's interest and not research programs. In reference to Australia, the only aquaponic research I know of was conducted at RMIT University (Royal Melbourne Institute of Technology) on the culture of Murray Cod in a lettuce aquaponic system with gravel substrate. The research was conducted recently by Dr. Wilson Lennard to obtain his Ph.D. degree.

➢ Student interested in research in aquaponics

Question

I am a high school student who has been researching and is interested in aquaponics. My goal is to find a new topic of research involved with aquaponics and then study it in school. I know that many people have come up with things that need to be researched and improved that are involved with aquaponics systems. Do you have any suggestions on a direction or starting place?

Answer

What needs to be researched is a problem I think about often as I design research projects. You are somewhat limited in high school by financial constraints and time, such as the length of the semester or school year. There are different types of aquaponic systems (e.g., nutrient film technique, raft or gravel) and, within these systems are different components. For example, solid waste can be removed by filters, settling tanks or not at all. There are also different types of fish and plants to be evaluated. The possibilities for research are endless. Right now at the University of the Virgin Islands we are doing an experiment with okra in our commercial-scale system. We are evaluating three varieties of okra and two planting densities and comparing production in the aquaponic system with production in soil, using a nearby field plot.

When using the scientific method, usually one variable is studied by testing two or three levels of that variable. For example, let's say you want to study the effect of fish stocking density on plant growth. The simplest way to do this is to set up two identical systems and vary the stocking rate. Maybe stock one system at the rate of one fish per gal and the other system at a rate of one fish per 2 gal. Feed the fish three times daily as much feed as they will consume in 30 minutes. Thereby one system should be getting twice as much feed and nutrient levels will be higher. Then you can see what effect higher nutrient levels have on plant growth and yield. You can also see the effect of a higher feeding rate on water quality. The two stocking rates are called treatments. Your treatments would be 1 fish/gal and 1 fish/2 gal.

In nature there is considerable variability so, if you get a difference, you cannot be sure this difference was due to the treatment or just natural variation. Therefore a proper scientific experiment would use at least three systems per treatment to obtain average values of growth rates, yields and water quality parameters. You can then analyze your data statistically to determine if the differences are real or just due to random variation. This type of research requires considerable resources which would not be available at a high school.

What I would suggest is that you build one good aquaponic system and evaluate the production of a fish species that is not usually raised in an aquaponic system. Perhaps you could buy ornamental fish or raise a wild fish species found in your state. Maybe you could catch small fingerlings by seining ponds. You will have to treat these fish very carefully to avoid problems with disease. A hardy fish species would be better. Then raise a plant that is not normally grown hydroponically, like we are doing with okra. Perhaps you could raise flowers or medicinal herbs. Document their growth and production carefully and measure water quality. I would also raise the same plants in soil, either outside or in greenhouse pots, to determine if they grow better in aquaponics. Our okra is growing at least five times faster in fish effluent than in soil. This is an excellent way of demonstrating the advantage of aquaponics. Good luck with your research.

➢ Algebra and geometry in aquaponics

Question

I need suggestions for the types of algebra and geometry problems students might need to solve when they are participating in various aquaponics and aquaculture activities. Do you have any suggestions?

Answer

The types of algebra and geometry problems encountered by the average fish farmer are quite simple. You need to determine the volume of circular-fish rearing tanks, rectangular hydroponic tanks and cylindro-conical clarifiers, which is a cylinder on top of a cone bottom with a particular slope (usually 45 or 60 degrees). Volume is important so you can determine how much of something must be added to achieve a certain concentration. We add chelated iron to our system every three weeks at a rate of 2 ppm (mg/liter), which are two ways of expressing the same concentration. You need to know the volume to determine how much iron to add.

The type of algebra used typically involves one unknown. Here is a sample problem: When fish approach a marketable size of 1.5 lbs (680 g), their feeding rate should be about 2% of body weight per day. If your filtration system can only treat the waste generated by 20 lbs (9.1 kg) of feed per day, how many fish should you stock?

Answer:
$(0.02)(x) = 20$ lbs.
$x = 20$ lbs./0.02
$x = 1,000$ lbs.
1000 lbs/1.5 lbs per fish $= 667$ fish

Now assume you have 90% survival
$(0.90)(x) = 667$ fish
$x = 667/0.90$
$x = 741$ fish

You would therefore stock 741 fish (or round up to 750 fish) so that you could reach a final weight of 1.5 lbs. while feeding optimally at 2% of body weight per day and not exceeding the filtration capacity (20 lbs. of feed) of your system.

A category of problems involving aquaculture in general

involves the conversion of English to metric units or vice versa. A student should come out of an aquaponics curriculum feeling comfortable in expressing production in lbs/gal or kg/m^3. There is a wide range of conversion problems (areas, volumes, flow rates, yields, etc.) that can be developed to reflect real-life situations. Students will benefit as scientists by learning both systems and moving freely between them.

➢ Going back to school for aquaponics

Question

I am seriously considering going back to school to earn a master's degree in aquaculture or aquaponics. What colleges and universities in the U.S. and Canada would have the best programs? I would prefer to concentrate in aquaponics if possible.

Answer

There are no schools offering aquaponic programs or degrees at this time. Many people have done research on aquaponics for their M.S. or Ph.D. degrees, but they have had to enroll in schools that offer degrees in aquaculture and then find a professor who is willing to let them do an aquaponic project for their research. You will most likely get direction in experimental design, fish husbandry and water quality, but you will have to do the aquaponics part by yourself. Placing a horticulturist or a civil engineer on your committee will provide additional needed expertise. This is how I did it at Auburn University. I am frequently asked to review aquaponic theses and dissertations, as an outside examiner, but this unfortunately is done after the research is complete and all I can do is critique or praise the final product. I suggest you find a good aquaculture program and a willing professor.

➤ Aquaponics in Japan

Question

I am a university student in Japan. I studied aquaponics at the University of Virgin Islands and I am continuing to study. Currently, I am writing a paper to be presented at the civil engineering meeting in Japan about aquaponics in the developing countries, developed countries and Japan. However, I have not found data about aquaponics in Japan. I am also looking for more data about the use of aquaponics in the developing countries and developed countries.

Could you tell me about data or sources for more data on aquaponics around the world?

Answer

It was pleasure having you in our class last year. It is good to hear that you are continuing the study of aquaponics. The best source of information on aquaponics is Aquaponics Journal. The latest information on aquaponic technology can be found here. I suggest you order back copies and contact the authors for additional information. The authors usually give their e-mail addresses. They could send you reprints of papers they published elsewhere or they could give you literature citations and you could obtain copies of articles through inter-library loan.

John Hargreaves and I published a literature review on aquaponics in 1993. Here is the citation for that article:

Rakocy, J.E. and J.A. Hargreaves. 1993. Integration of vegetable hydroponics with fish culture: a review. Pages 112-136 in J.K. Wang, editor. Proceedings of the Aquaculture Engineering Conference on Techniques for Modern Aquaculture. Aquacultural Engineering Group, American Society of Agricultural Engineers.

This paper reports on all the aquaponic research we could find in the literature up to that time. In 1994 I published a paper in a

Japanese journal. The paper was presented at a meeting which was held in Japan. Here is the citation for that paper:

Rakocy, J.E. 1994. Waste management in integrated recirculating systems. Proceedings of the 21st United States-Japan Meeting on Aquaculture. Bulletin of National Research Institute of Aquaculture, Supplement 1:75-80.

Aquaponics is new to Japan and there is probably no research data on Japanese aquaponics in the literature yet. A couple years ago a film crew from Japan visited UVI, Bioshelters and a few other facilities to make a documentary on aquaponics, which was shown on Japanese television to an estimated audience of 5 million viewers. I am sure this documentary has sparked interest in aquaponics which should lead to research and commercial development in Japan.

There has been little or no work on aquaponics in developing countries. It is an area of research that needs to be addressed. I believe a country has to be developed to the extent that it is economically feasible to use pumps, aerators and fish feed. Many countries cannot afford these items and rely on pond culture with agricultural byproducts and manure as the only inputs. Perhaps aquaponics would be more feasible near the large population centers of developing countries where land is scarce and high value products can be raised for the middle and upper classes or for export markets.

➤ Trial using NFT

Question

I am studying for the Advanced Diploma of Horticulture Production at the University of Melbourne in Australia. After discovering aquaponics while doing an assignment last year, I have become very interested in doing a trial. I have several mini NFT systems on hand that grow 18 plants and a 60L reservoir to go with each of them. I am planning on growing lettuce in these kits. I have sourced out some fish from a local pet shop (barramundi, silver perch and Murray cod) and was wondering if you could help me out with a few questions that I have.

> *Which of these species do you think would be best for an initial trial?*
> *How many fish (1 - 2 inches in size) will be necessary in the systems I have?*
> *What pH is preferable for the fish?*
> *What is the best type of fish feed to produce the best type of effluent?*

Answer

Barramundi and Murray cod have been grown successfully in aquaponic systems. I am not familiar with silver perch, but I heard this fish mentioned as a possible candidate for aquaponics. I suggest starting with barramundi as there is interest in culturing this species in temperate regions in heated closed recirculating systems.

The design ratio is based on the daily feed input per unit of plant growing area. In raft hydroponics the design ratio varies from 60 to 100 g of fish feed per m^2 of plant growing area per day. In an aquaponic system using nutrient film technique (NFT), there is approximately 50% less water if all the other components remain the same size. Therefore, the design ratio should be approximately 30-50 g/m^2/day. I would use the lower ratio because there is less surface area in an NFT system for biofiltration. I know from research at UVI that optimum leaf lettuce density is 16 plants/m^2, which is roughly equivalent to the number of plants that your system can grow. However, the surface area of your NFT troughs is probably lower. You should measure it. It will be a faction of 1 m^2. Multiply this fraction by 30 g. The product will be the average daily fish feeding rate. To illustrate, I will assume the plant growing area in your system is 0.5 m^2. You should therefore stock the rearing tank with enough fingerlings to consume 15 g of feed per day.

The fish stocking rate should result in final harvest density is 60 kg/m^3 (0.5 lbs/gal). This is equivalent to 3.6 kg (7.9 lbs) in your rearing tank, which is 0.06 m^3 (15.8 gal). If you raised the fish to a final size of 500 g (1.1 lbs), you would stock about seven fish. Assume that the total weight of the seven fingerlings, 1-2 inches in length, is negligible and that the total weight gain of all the fish is 3.6 kg. Assuming that the feed conversion ratio is 1.7 (1.7 lbs of feed produces 1 lb of fish gain), total feed consumption over a 6-month (180 days) growing period would be 6.1 kg or 6,100 g. Dividing total feed consumption by 180 days equals an average of 34 g of feed per day.

Tackling this problem from both the plant and fish perspectives shows that the average daily feeding rate should be in the range of 15-34 g. With one small fish rearing tank, I suggest you use batch culture, which means that all the fish would be stocked at one time and cultured for 180 days. Feed input to the system will increase over time. Therefore, in the beginning there may be insufficient nutrients for good plant growth while at the end there may be excess nutrients, which could be toxic to the plants. One month is required after stocking for establishment of bacteria in the biofilter (tank surface areas including NFT troughs). During this period the fish must be underfed (do not feed them as much as they want to eat), and there will not be enough nutrient accumulation for plant growth. Plants can be added at the beginning of the second month. In the latter part of the trial, nutrient levels may become too high (exceeding 2,000 ppm as total dissolved solids). A small meter can be purchased which easily measures TDS. Good plant growth generally occurs in the range of 200-2,000 ppm. If TDS exceeds 2,000 ppm, it can be decreased by exchanging some of the culture water with new water. You should install a glass wool filter to remove suspended solids from the stream of water that you pump to the NFT troughs.

pH should be maintained in the range of 7.0-7.5 by alternately adding calcium hydroxide and potassium hydroxide. Small amounts should be added on a regular (almost daily) basis. Chelated iron should be added once every 3 weeks at a concentration of 2 ppm. Use a complete diet (containing all required minerals and vitamins) of floating pellets with a minimum of 32% protein. The species you select may require higher protein levels. Ask your local aquaculture extension agent for help in selecting the best available feed. I recommend feeding *ad libitum* (as much as they can consume to 30 minutes) two to three times daily.

I have made many assumptions. The figures I have given you are in the ballpark, but you will have to do some trial and error work to optimize your system.

References

Recirculating Aquaculture Tank Production Systems: Aquaponics – Integrating Fish and Plant Culture
James E. Rakocy, Michael P. Masser and Thomas M. Losordo
Southern Regional Aquaculture Center, Publication No. 454
https://srac.tamu.edu/index.cfm/event/getFactSheet/whichfactsheet/105/

Hydroponic Food Production, fifth edition
Dr. Howard M. Resh
http://www.howardresh.com/Howard-Resh-Books.html

University of California Good Agriculture Practices (GAP), Eliminate Fecal Coliforms from Your Vegetable and Fruit Safety Vocabulary
University of California, Agriculture and Natural Resources.
http://groups.ucanr.org/UC_GAPs/Elimanate_Fecal_Coliforms/

Sanitary Standard Operating Procedures (SSOP)
Food and Drug Administration
http://www.access.gpo.gov/nara/cfr/waisidx_03/21cfr110_03.html

An Integrated Fish and Field Crop System for Arid Areas
James E. Rakocy
pages 263-286, Ecological Aquaculture: The Evolution of the Blue Revolution, Barry A. Costa-Pierce, editor, 2002, Blackwell Science.

Integration of vegetable hydroponics with fish culture: a review
James E. Rakocy, John A. Hargreaves. 1993.
Pages 112-136, Proceedings of the Aquaculture Engineering Conference on Techniques for Modern Aquaculture. Aquacultural Engineering Group, American Society of Agricultural Engineers.

Cultured Aquatic Species Information, Oreochromis niloticus
Fisheries and Agriculture Dept, FAO, United Nations
http://www.fao.org/fishery/culturedspecies/Oreochromis_niloticus/en

Aquaponics Journal, 1997 – 2011, Issues 1-60
www.aquaponicsjournal.com